Artfulness

Formula-Free Creative Writing Explorations for Secondary ELA Classes

ANDREA YARBOUGH

A Writing Wednesday Book

For teachers everywhere, who dedicate their lives to improving the lives of their students.

Alexandrite Publishing, LLC
www.alexandritepublishing.com

Cover design: Kevin Yarbough
Index: Heather Pendley

First Edition May 2022

ISBN 979-8-9860146-0-9 (paperback)

Library of Congress Control Number: 2022905806

Printed in the United States of America

Acknowledgments

When I first began my teaching career, I never dreamed I would someday write an educator resource. Of course, I also never dreamed that I would be fortunate enough to work with such an amazing group of teachers. The entire English department at Patriot High School, both past and present, has shaped my development and I owe them a debt of gratitude for sharing their expertise and their friendship.

Our department thrives under the leadership of DeLores Lucas and Bobbi Scott. Literally, the first educator to believe in me, DeLores has supported me every step of my career. And as our department chair, Bobbi has always led by example, offering her support and guidance every single day. It is because of these two incredible women and their invaluable mentorship that I had the knowledge and the courage to write this book.

In addition, I would like to thank my principal, Dr. Michael Bishop, and Prince William County Schools for fostering an environment that encourages teachers to thrive.

I must also recognize Patti Napolitano who was the first to introduce me to the power of creative writing in core ELA classes and whose company kept me sane as we worked together toward National Board certification and Adrienne Phillips who was a terrific mentor to me as I began this journey.

No book would be possible without a team of experts, including my proofreader and indexer, Heather Pendley of Pendley's Pro Editing & Indexing and two of my oldest friends, Kat Aragon and Patty Winske of LimeLife by Alcone, as well as Luis Aragon of Luis Aragon Photography, all of whom so generously offered their expertise in beauty and photography to ensure that I looked picture-perfect for my author's image.

Thanks are also in order to my parents who encouraged me to always do my best and my sister, Valerie, who is often among the first people to "like" my posts on social media.

To my children, who patiently allowed me to brainstorm lesson ideas with them, forgave me when I disappeared into the hole of my computer for days on end, and helped me get my very first sale, I cannot express how much I appreciate and love you.

But perhaps the person who has been the most instrumental in getting this book into your hands is my best friend and husband, Kevin Yarbough, whose knowledge and patience cannot be understated. Since I first began contemplating this book, Kevin has been cheering me on, encouraging me when I faltered, and offering his help in just about every way possible to ensure I could succeed.

To everyone who has played a role along my journey—thank you! This book would not be possible without each and every one of you, and I am so grateful to have you in my life.

Table of Contents

1
Chapter

Look Inside Chapter 1

SCAN ME

Scan to access
supplemental
resources

When people learn of my book, I am often greeted with two seemingly contradictory responses: at first, excitement. A year's worth of standards-aligned creative writing plans ready to go on day one—yes, please! Then, trepidation. A year's worth of creative writing plans . . . As in, dedicating one full instructional day a week to . . . creative writing? In a core English class . . . ?

It appears that creative writing is so ingrained in our minds as an elective that it's hard to imagine, as core English Language Arts (ELA) instructors, dedicating an entire day each week to the task. *How*, we ask ourselves, *will we ever get to the "real" content if we are spending so much time on creative writing?* The question we should be asking ourselves, however, is why we don't consider creative writing to be part of our core instruction in the first place.

As Secondary ELA teachers, we are tasked with providing instruction for both literacy and composition skills. However, if we're being honest with ourselves, we know that, for many of us, literacy skills are given higher priority in our classrooms. The composition skills we do incorporate are often in the service of literacy skills; we teach an analytical essay, for example, primarily to measure a student's ability to analyze a text rather than to measure their ability to compose a quality text of their own.

Researcher Steve Graham digs into this issue deeper in "Changing How Writing is Taught." When reflecting on his findings from 28 academic studies on the subject of writing instruction, Graham notes that "The overall picture that emerged . . .was that writing instruction in most classrooms is not sufficient. One indicator of this inadequacy was that the majority of teachers did not devote enough time to teaching writing." He further finds that, most frequently, the writing tasks assigned to students "involved very little extended writing" and that "students were seldom asked to write text that was a paragraph or longer." Graham is careful to observe that the findings indicate a variety of factors that lead to these outcomes, including large class sizes and pressures on time, which we all know from experience have negative consequences on our ability to integrate a range of academic best practices. The purpose of pointing out these findings here is not to suggest that teachers are in any way failing in their duties to their students, but to simply confirm what many of us instinctively know: our current approach to writing instruction, as it is often taught in our classrooms, is insufficient.

This book does not aim to address all the causes of this insufficiency, nor is it designed as a panacea that will magically overcome all of the challenges we face in our daily lives. What this book is designed to do, however, is to help teachers integrate lengthy and more frequent writing into our regular instruction—precisely the two areas that Graham finds are lacking in the secondary classroom.

But now the next question: why *creative* writing? *Why not something meatier*, you might ask, *like persuasion or expository writing?* Quite simply, students respond to creative writing. A recent Pew Research study, "Writing, Technology and Teens," found that "teens who enjoy their school writing more are more likely to engage in creative writing at school compared to teens who report very little enjoyment of school writing (81% vs. 69%)." Furthermore, creative writing is inherently writer-focused, allowing the writer to experiment with their writing in ways that more structured writing tasks do not. Pulitzer Prize-winning journalist Donald Murray cautions: "When you give [students] an assignment you tell [them] what to say and how to say it, and thereby cheat your student[s] of the opportunity to learn the process of discovery we call writing." Rather than assigning a particular focus or format, he argues, we should be teaching "unfinished writing, and glory in its unfinishedness" (13). The lessons contained in this book aim to do just that, providing a safe space for students to experiment with writing in ways that formal writing tasks often prevent. And because the tools needed to write creatively are the same tools needed to write for other purposes, creative writing activities can be used to teach transferrable skills such as narrative nonfiction, voice, syntax, diction, and organization. What's more, well-designed creative writing lessons can be used to target literacy skills as well, teaching students how to become better readers by engaging them in the process of better

writing. A glance at Common Core standards for English Language Arts, the educational standards that are set at the national level, for example, reveals that creative writing tasks align clearly with many of the required reading strands. Here is just a small sampling of the language:

- "Analyze the cumulative impact of specific word choices on meaning and tone."

- "Analyze how an author's choices concerning how to structure a text, order events within it (e.g., parallel plots), and manipulate time (e.g., pacing, flashbacks) create such effects as mystery, tension, or surprise."

- "Analyze how an author draws on and transforms source material in a specific work." (National Governors Association Center for Best Practices & Council of Chief State School Officers, Grades 9-10)

Notice how in these three strands, which Common Core lists under the reading standards, what the skill is actually targeting is an understanding of the *construction* of the text: why an author selected a particular word or set of words, how the structural choices shape meaning, where the author drew inspiration. The emphasis is not on the text itself, but on authorial choices and the impact of those choices on meaning. But now let's explore how this skill is commonly taught in classrooms all around the country.

At the beginning of the year, teachers meet in their Collaborative Learning Teams to develop a Pacing Guide for the year, exploring the standards they are expected to teach in their grade level and then developing a scaffolded structure that ensures they hit all of the required skills by the end of the year. As part of this planning, teachers select the texts that they are either required to teach or that they feel best fit any given standard. At the designated point in the year, the whole class engages in a reading of that text, carefully annotating in the margins, working in small groups to explore meaning, and finally, expressing their understanding in a literary analysis essay that demonstrates how well they understood what the author was attempting to do.

So far so good, right? But a question remains, and it's a question that I admittedly failed to ask myself for most of my early teaching years: how, exactly, are students supposed to determine the effect of any given authorial choice if they've never had to grapple with the consequences of those choices themselves? If they've never had to determine the effect of swapping out the word "may" with the word "must," for example, or choose between setting X or setting Y when developing their own story, how can they possibly understand the significance of another author making those same choices?

For many students, the answer is simple: they can't. And we know they can't because their literary analysis essays often hover on superficial explorations, summarizing the moves the author is making rather than analyzing the effect of those moves on the reader's understanding of the text. But the effect of those moves on the reader's understanding of the text is *exactly* what the Common Core standards expect us to teach. By only teaching students to explore these moves in other people's writing, we limit their ability to truly understand the significance of choice in the writing process.

The idea that students need to do more than simply read good literature to become good readers is not new. It is also important for them to grapple with constructing good writing themselves, learning through experience that writing is a process before it is a product, recognizing through their own attempts at writing the effects of various techniques on meaning. Linda Flowers and John Hayes elaborate on this idea in their article, "Problem Solving Strategies and the Writing Process."

> Because the act of writing is a complex cognitive skill, not a body of knowledge, teaching writers to analyze the product [the finished novel, for example] often fails to intervene at a meaningful stage in the writer's performance. Such teaching leaves a gap because it has little to say about the techniques and thinking process of writing as a student (or anyone else) experience. (450)

It is clear that, if we seek to strengthen literacy and critical thinking skills in our classrooms, we need to incorporate more than just reading (and writing about reading) into the core curriculum. Students need to write. Frequently.

The Power of Writing Wednesdays

Including more frequent writing opportunities into our classroom serves multiple academic purposes. In a world where communication forms and genres are constantly evolving, we have a responsibility as educators to teach our students as much as we possibly can about incorporating thoughtful and deliberate choices into their writing. When is it appropriate to craft a blog instead of an image-based social media post, for example, or what is a listicle and how can it be used to target a particular communication goal? When we contain our writing instruction primarily to literary analysis, we spend all of our energy teaching students to write in a genre that few students, if any, will actually use in their future and we teach them that writing only takes one form, serves one purpose, and is crafted in one voice. Is it any wonder that students groan the moment we introduce a writing task to them? By the time they get to high school, any joy students may have ever felt for writing has been eliminated one five-paragraph essay at a time.

Unlike the formulaic structures often used to teach essay writing, Writing Wednesday lessons offer opportunities for students to engage in diverse writing styles, experiment with narrative voices, play around with organization and genre. Because their drafts are shared with others but not graded, students are motivated to produce good work, but not pressured to produce flawless work. As a result, students are more willing to take risks, trying new techniques with their writing that they would hesitate to attempt if they knew they might lose points for their effort.

This past school year, I introduced our first Writing Wednesday activity on the second day of class. Introducing the lessons so early in the year was not without risks. Would students be prepared and willing to write on day two? Would they be able to sustain writing for the length of time the lesson required? Was I going to inadvertently start us off on the wrong foot by beginning with an activity they might feel unprepared for?

Figure 1.1 Students explore portrait art during the *Express Yourself* lesson.

Trusting the process, I ignored my fears and pushed forward. The response from students was overwhelmingly positive. On only the second day of class, all of my students were engaged and actively writing. As **Figure 1.1** shows, students began that day's lesson, *Express Yourself,* by rotating to various art stations around the room. The anticipatory activity served as a great natural ice breaker as students began instinctively working together and sharing observations while they wandered. This opening activity set the tone for all of our future work, allowing students to collaborate with one another on their own terms. When the anticipatory activity concluded, they returned to their seats

Figure 1.2 Students actively engage in writing on their second instructional day of the year.

and began writing. I wrote with them, occasionally lifting my head to see how they were doing, secretly worried they may start to lose steam too quickly. Imagine my surprise when, not only did all of the students continue writing for the

remainder of the lesson, but they actually groaned when I warned them their time was almost up! (See **Figure 1.2**)

These results were not anomalous, repeating themselves time after time in class after class. Since the Writing Wednesday launch that first week of school, student feedback has been consistently positive. Some Writing Teams have asked about the theme for upcoming Celebration Days well in advance so they can begin planning early. Student reflections reveal Writing Wednesdays are among their favorite class activities. One student even thanked me for the lessons, writing: "they made me realize writing fiction would be my dream job . . ." The excitement most students feel for Writing Wednesdays is hard to deny. But simply being motivated to complete a task does not necessarily mean that task has educational value. So, beyond increasing student engagement, what's the power of Writing Wednesdays?

The real power of Writing Wednesdays is that, by encouraging students to see themselves as Writers, to see that their voices matter, students begin to recognize the control they have over their own writing, and they begin to see the value in exploring other strong examples of writing in an effort to strengthen their own craft. In other words, Writing Wednesdays create an intrinsic motivation for students that affects their engagement both with writing and reading lessons.

Connection to Core Instruction

I hadn't always appreciated the value of creative writing in a core ELA class, however. When I first began integrating structured creative writing tasks into my classes, I considered those lessons to be fun little detours from our regular instruction. The kinds of lessons that were great to include on the day before a long break—academic but not necessarily important. In short, I considered creative writing lessons to be optional.

As I began reflecting on my instruction, however, it became clear that creative writing lessons had far more impact on my students than I ever anticipated. *Why*, I found myself wondering, *should lessons that clearly*

> Inspired by the work of Felicia Rose Chavez, Celebration Days are instructional days in which we celebrate student writing via a Writer's showcase.

8

encourage students to blossom, be relegated to "lame duck" days? Was there a way for the creative writing lessons to become more targeted? Better aligned to core instruction? To answer these questions, I sat down and began lesson planning. For days and days, weeks and weeks, I poured over the academic strands, the book units, the pacing guides. I thought about what types of skills we needed to target and how creative writing lessons could be aligned with those skills. And when I was finished, I had a year's worth of creative writing lessons that were each designed to target specific, core ELA skills. And they were designed to easily integrate into any larger instructional unit.

At the beginning of the year, for example, my sophomores were reading a passage from Edgar Allan Poe's, "The Fall of the House of Usher" to explore how literary elements, such as setting, shaped meaning. When Wednesday rolled around, I adapted the lesson, *Roll the Dice*, to emphasize setting. The connection between the literature unit and the writing lesson was deliberate: students first analyzed Poe's development of setting by closely reading a passage taken from the beginning of the narrative. Then, they were asked to write their own setting-forward original story.

As part of their reading exploration, they were asked to consider whether Poe might become a mentor author for them—a writer whose work inspires them to attempt a specific technique or approach in their own writing. Results were mixed. Some students disliked the style choices Poe employed as his narrator described the crumbling house. These students realized, perhaps for the first time, that their own writing style tends to favor different syntax structures or specific narrative techniques. Other students fell in love with Poe's technique, taking note of how his layering of details suggests, without directly stating, the foreboding presence of an otherwise grand home. These students then made concentrated efforts, as shown in the sample self-reflections provided in **Figure 1.3**, to attempt a similar approach in their own writing. Regardless of how they felt about Poe's style, both groups of students thought critically about the impact of his authorial choices and then considered how their understanding of authorial

choice affected the understanding and development of their own Writer's Voice. By pairing the literary analysis component—how did Poe's approach to setting shape understanding?—with an exploration of their own writing style, students had not one but two opportunities to engage thoughtfully with the text, becoming both better readers and writers in the process.

Will Poe become a Mentor Writer?   ☐ Yes   ☒ No

Why or why not? Be specific.

His pacing is too shoa/clipped and his word choice huas my brain. I also dont like 1st person.

Will Poe become a Mentor Writer?   ☑ Yes   ☐ No

Why or why not? Be specific.

~~I think its description of the setting is too specific in depth.~~ I changed my mind. I actually love Poe's word choice & the mood set by it. I also like darker stories, because happily ever after is unrealistic.

I chose this piece because molding this work together with my teammates created a story with different aspects of each writer. However, even though different people put their work together to create a new story, setting and wording was very similar. Although Edgar Allen Poe's work is not my favorite, his work with conveying a dark mood through vocabulary and imagery influence how I wrote my piece. From my first draft, I needed to remove the science fiction elements and instead of focusing characters, my edited version was broadly focused on the city to add a sense of ambiguity. I believe my published piece included a lot of specific wording and tone to create a detailed image, it also has many elements of mystery to hook the reader. In the future, I

---

3. The mentor that influenced me to write this piece was Edgar Allen Poe. I tried to channel the sort of unhinged narration that he often does when he writes in first person. Many of his stories I've read have been eerie and at times gruesome, so I wanted to channel that scary first person into my writing. I also feel like in some of his stories I've read, they start out slow, and the person tends to grow impatient or angry and the buildup happens, as they get angrier, or more paranoid they confess to something or do something without thinking.

Figure 1.3 Evaluating Poe as a mentor author.

Notice in the above example how Writing Wednesday tasks serve to link reading instruction to some larger purpose. When texts are explored in isolation—books that are read simply to explore authors' craft—the majority of our students struggle to find a purpose in the study. While our natural readers may love the book units, the average student finds themself wondering what the point is. And they're not wrong for doing so. If students have no intention of going on to college-level literature study, recognizing and understanding how literary elements serve to shape meaning solely for the sake of recognizing and understanding how literary elements serve to shape meaning seems completely pointless—exactly the kind of "school learning" that many adults complain has no impact on their real lives.

By turning book units into an opportunity to hone their own writer's craft, however, and allowing them to write in formats and genres that are authentic to the real world, we are encouraging students to see the value of literary studies. As showcased in the earlier example, by recognizing the impact of a layered approach to setting, students can determine whether they find that particular approach reflective of their own Writer's Voice.

Now, some of you may be thinking that exploring books from a thematic approach also serves to overcome objections by our reluctant readers. If we can show them how any given book connects to the real world, we are providing them with a motivation for reading. And this is certainly true. However, while a thematic study of literature does an excellent job of allowing students to consider how storytelling helps them understand their world, it does far less in helping them become both critical thinkers and strong communicators. Writing Wednesdays, on the other hand, can target all of these tasks simultaneously.

- *Thematic Study:* Writing Wednesdays provide opportunities for students to explore a common theme via their own writing, thereby connecting any book unit to something meaningful in their lives. In addition, several of the Writing Wednesday activities can be adapted to include paired texts in a variety

of genres—poetry, art, music—that can incorporate an overarching theme topic.

- *Critical Thinking:* Because Writing Wednesdays do not rely upon formulas, students have to engage in critical thinking to determine how best to approach any given writing task. *What will be the impact,* they must ask, *of selecting this genre over that genre, or this setting over that setting?* Not only do students begin thinking about authorial choices in their writing, but they become more sensitive to authorial choices in the text units as well.

- *Communication Skills:* Writing Wednesdays require thoughtfulness. Whether students have to determine which medium to communicate in (written, visual, oral . . .) or which genre to select (social media, blog, essay . . .), Writing Wednesdays force students to think about how best to achieve their communication goal for any given audience. Assigning students the responsibility to make many of these choices themselves shifts the burden of learning from the teacher to the student and, over time, results in students becoming both stronger—and more confident—communicators.

Endlessly adaptive, Writing Wednesday lessons do not stop at integration into the core curriculum, however. They also provide opportunities to extend learning across a range of skills. To continue to support core instruction beyond the Writing Wednesday lesson, each activity in this book includes suggestions for teachers to expand student learning further. From vocabulary to research, literary analysis to multimedia presentations, each lesson is designed both to integrate with and extend core instruction across a range of communication skills.

Culturally Responsive

Encouraging students to become stronger and more confident communicators is one of many positive outcomes Writing Wednesdays promote. This is because Writing Wednesday lessons are specifically written to be student-focused. With an increasingly diverse student population, it is imperative that our lessons allow all students to flourish. That is why every activity is designed to be culturally responsive.

Much has been made in the media lately about culturally responsive pedagogy. There is a lot of confusing and sometimes misleading information about what it means when teachers include culturally responsive activities in their lessons. For the purposes of this book, "culturally responsive instruction" is defined as instruction that is designed to support and respect every learner in the classroom in a way that recognizes their unique backgrounds, talents, and interests. All Writing Wednesday activities support culturally responsive learning in the following ways:

- By allowing students to self-select the direction their narratives take, including the freedom to experiment with genre, voice, and style

- By placing students into Writing Teams that promote a sense of community through supportive collaboration

- By incorporating Celebration Days which provide all students an opportunity to showcase the best of their writing

In addition, many of the Writing Wednesday activities allow teachers the opportunity to celebrate the unique backgrounds of their students or broaden students' understanding of the world through carefully curated paired resources. Some lessons, for example, include mentor texts which can be thoughtfully selected to highlight a variety of genres or writing voices. Others include sample art pieces that can be pulled from widely available open source resources, found within the local community at art museums or galleries, or even by visiting with the school's art teacher and finding samples from the students themselves. Incorporating culturally responsive strategies into each lesson increases students' ability to develop authentic—as opposed to formulaic—Writer's Identities and ensures that our instruction is designed to reflect and support all learners equally.

Beginning the Journey

Artfulness makes getting started with Writing Wednesdays simple. The easiest way to begin is to simply follow the sequence laid out in the book, moving from lesson to lesson as each quarter progresses. That being said, I strongly recommend that you spend a little time before you begin integrating Writing Wednesdays into your instruction to review each of the lessons in order to familiarize yourself with the range of options provided in the text. This is also a good time to explore the ways each lesson can be both integrated into larger units and extended beyond that day's lesson. Compare the lessons to the units you will be teaching and determine the best sequence for your classes. Make sure you set aside a few days near the end of each quarter for students to work in class on their Celebration Day assessments.

You may have fewer Writing Wednesday days available in any given quarter than there are Writing Wednesday lesson plans. If that happens, select the lessons that you believe will benefit your students the most that quarter and simply omit the extra lessons. Then, be sure to adjust the Celebration Day instructions accordingly.

In addition, familiarizing yourself with the key terminology and process for the lessons will help ensure that integration of the lessons is both seamless and effective. See **Figure 1.4** for a quick explanation of the key terms you will find in the lessons.

Figure 1.4

Writing Wednesday Key Terminology:

Celebration Days: Classroom expo designed to showcase Writers' work (Chavez).

As the name implies, these are days when the class comes together to celebrate the work of individual Writers and their Teams. The more you lean into the Celebration Day format (with decorations, food, etc.), the more students will relax and enjoy each other as Writers rather than focus on the more competitive elements of education they often prioritize during assessments. Their work for these days is ultimately designed to be assessed, but the focus during class time is on celebrating their growth as Writers rather than critiquing their work. Any areas in need of attention going forward can be identified in the private assessment comments they receive later on.

Observations: For any given Writing Wednesday lesson, the section of their drafting page where they make observations connected to the lesson.

Many of the Writing Wednesday lessons include opening activities that are designed to get students thinking critically about the upcoming task. Often, students are asked to keep track of their initial thoughts by taking notes in the Observation section of their Writer's Notebook. This portion of their Notebook is placed directly below the header of that day's activity (which also includes the date and title of the lesson). When they are ready to draft, they will do so beneath the Observation section of that day's lesson.

Figure 1.4 Continued

Publication Piece: Final versions of student drafts, usually submitted for grading.

The work students do during the weekly lessons is intended as draft work only. There is no expectation that any particular draft will ever be taken through additional revisions. However, each quarter, students will be expected to select at least one of their draft pieces to purposefully revise into a Publication Piece which will be showcased during the Celebration Day activities. Publication Pieces are polished works that students have had time to bring through multiple rounds of revision and, ideally, have had a chance to further improve through peer or teacher conferences.

Writers: As used throughout *Artfulness*, student writers.

You will notice throughout the book that I refer to the students as Writers with a capital "W." This is by design as it is used to define students as thoughtful, deliberate Writers who understand the power they hold to communicate with others effectively. *Writer's Identity* and *Writer's Voice* carry similar meanings, with an emphasis on each student's unique sense of style.

Writer's Notebook: The notebook where each student's draft writing will live.

At the beginning of the year, ask students to obtain a Writer's Notebook that is used *exclusively* for Writing Wednesday activities. Periodically, you will see "Writer's Notebook" shortened to "Notebook." It is important that students understand the difference between a journal, which is usually intended to capture personal reflections, and an academic notebook, which should carry no expectation of privacy and should be filled with targeted writing explorations based on each assigned activity.

Writing Teams: Groups of students who will work together during Writing Wednesday lessons and related activities; usually composed of three to four students per Team.

Ideally, these Teams will stay constant throughout the year to develop a stronger sense of community within each Team. Periodically, you will see "Writing Teams" shortened to "Teams" for stylistic reasons. Most Writing Wednesday lessons envision students sitting with their Writing Team while working and then sharing their drafts with them for guided feedback at the end of each lesson.

Writing Wednesdays: Based upon the lessons contained in texts identified by Alexandrite Publishing, LLC, as "A Writing Wednesday Book," these are instructional days dedicated entirely to the craft of writing.

Throughout the book, you may sometimes see the lessons contained in this book referred to as "Writing Wednesday" lessons. This term simply signals that we are discussing one or more of the lessons contained within this book or other books in the Writing Wednesday series. While the day of the week reserved for these lessons is somewhat arbitrary, the alliteration allows students to easily remember that Wednesdays are writing days, and it allows them to anticipate the lessons they will encounter when they arrive at class. You are, of course, encouraged to select the day of the week that works best for your own instructional needs, but I do recommend selecting a fixed writing day each week so students are able to establish a predictable routine.

Writing Teams

Providing students with regular opportunities to develop their writing skills is a key premise of this book. However, as a teacher myself, I recognize the near impossibility of providing meaningful feedback on all of the drafts our students will be producing as part of the Writing Wednesday lessons. Acknowledging this struggle, educator and author Kelly Gallagher nonetheless argues that "students need to be writing way more than a teacher can grade" ("Moving Beyond the 4x4 Classroom"). The challenge I'd found in my own classes, however, is that when students realize their work will not receive a score, they simply choose not to complete it. Writing Teams seem to have resolved this issue. By providing students with a built-in audience to whom they are responsible, students are compelled to produce something of relative quality to share with their peers. Not only does the Writing Team format address concerns of motivation for writing, but creating an environment where their writing is shared with their peers but not graded allows students to thrive by encouraging them to take risks they would otherwise hesitate to take.

Although the lessons contained in this book often ask students to share with Writing Teams before completing the individual reflection, you may wish to reverse this sequence for your students so they can use the findings from their reflection to request targeted feedback from their Writing Team.

So what is a "Writing Team?" Reflecting the work of educators like Gretchen Hovan and Felicia Rose Chavez, Writing Wednesday lessons root each individual Writer into a larger Writing Team, a group of students with whom they will work closely for the remainder of the year. These Teams are meant to be supportive, not competitive. At the end of most lessons, students are asked to share their writing with their Team members by reading their work aloud exactly as it was written. After each student has shared their work, the Team members engage in discussions designed to reflect on the learning process and to celebrate the "wins" of each day's work while brainstorming the next steps with fellow Writers rather than telling their classmates what they need to "fix" to improve their writing.

Building Community

Many teachers are understandably concerned about requiring their students to share their writing aloud with their peers. There are many good reasons for these concerns, including consideration for students who are shy or introverted, worry about the stress oral readings may cause for students who struggle with anxiety, and concerns about how to respect the range of cultural backgrounds our students may bring to the classroom. I, too, was worried about all of these factors when I first began my Writing Wednesday journey. Addressing these concerns and showing respect for all of my students was of paramount importance as I designed the lessons. I found the solution in the Writing Teams format.

Although students are often hesitant to share their work with the entire class, particularly early in the school year, the smaller, more intimate nature of Writing Teams seems to alleviate many of the concerns students initially express. In my own classes, not only have I experienced a remarkably high participation rate within the Writing Teams, I have even overheard students arriving at class eager to share writing they completed outside of class with their Team members, recognizing their Team members as valuable participants along their own Writer's journey, regardless of whether their writing was assigned or developed independently.

There are some key steps I recommend to maximize the success of your Writing Teams:

- Keep the Writing Teams small, ideally between three or four students per Team.

- Determine whether you want students to select their Writing Teams or whether you want to assign students into Teams yourself. There are advantages and disadvantages to both approaches. Having older students in my own classes, I elected to allow them to choose their own Writing Teams. I did, however, wait until they had a chance to get to know their classmates a little before they selected their Teams, and I cautioned them that, except in cases of severe dysfunction, they were expected to stay in their Teams for the entire year. So far, the only

adjustments I've made to the Teams were caused by students transferring into or out of my classes once the school year was under way.

- ✒ Tell students *in advance* that they will be sharing their writing both aloud and verbatim with their Team members. It would be unfair to ask students to share work with others that they initially wrote with the expectation of privacy. (Students should, however, have the option to skip small passages if they prefer to keep certain portions private).

- ✒ Provide Teams with guidance on the structure and purpose of the Team share so that they are focused on providing growth-oriented feedback for each Writer in a manner that is supportive of that Writer's Identity and Voice.

The Writer's Notebook

Ensuring students have a consistent location to draft their writing is another important step in the process. I recommend having students write their creations by hand in a dedicated notebook, which many educators call a Writer's Notebook.

When introducing students to Writing Wednesday activities, I encourage you to spend some time discussing their Writer's Notebook with them to clarify expectations. In my own classes, for example, we spend a few minutes exploring the differences between a journal and a notebook until students come to understand that, whereas journaling is more personal and reflective in nature, the Writer's Notebook is academic and should be considered as such when they write. We also discuss the reasons why having a dedicated Writer's Notebook is important. It allows them to keep all of their work in one easy-to-find location, review and evaluate their growth over time, and more clearly organize their learning in an effective manner by keeping a notebook that is dedicated exclusively to creative writing.

You always have the option to adjust where student writing lives. These days, there are certainly good arguments to be made for having a digital, as opposed to a handwritten Notebook, including storing and accessing student work with ease, eliminating concerns over legibility, and saving paper. However, writing by hand is an entirely different experience than typing. There is something about having the ability to move the pen across the page in any direction one desires, scratching out words with purpose rather than simply "erasing" them from the screen, drawing arrows to linked ideas or even doodling as one brainstorms that frees students from the confines of writing "correctly" or "neatly" and allows them to simply . . . write. This is why, in my classes, our Writer's Notebook remains paper-based.

Drafting

During each Writing Wednesday lesson, students will draft their work in their Writer's Notebook. The wonderful thing about the Writer's Notebook is that none of the work contained in this Notebook is graded. Not one single piece. Why is that important? Because it allows students to take risks with their writing in ways they otherwise would not. Their Writer's Notebook essentially becomes an experimental laboratory full of trial and error. In their Writer's Notebook, students can flex their creative muscles, trying on different voices and genres, different structures and techniques. Some of their experiments will work. Many will not. Either way, students learn.

It is also important, however, that these drafts serve some larger objective. Absent an authentic audience and an opportunity to eventually produce something meaningful, students would come to see Writing Wednesday lessons as busy-work that simply occupies time. Ensuring they have both an audience and a purpose are of paramount importance.

To encourage students to produce meaningful work during the drafting stage, even when those drafts are in their roughest form, most Writing Wednesday activities conclude with a Team reading and a self-reflection. Sharing with their Team members provides Writers with an authentic audience for their earliest attempts, giving them a chance to get feedback and support at this early stage. The self-reflection allows them to think critically about the connection between their goal and

their approach, thereby forcing them to recognize the role of authorial choice in developing meaning. The Team share and the self-reflection component are designed to provide students with an authentic audience and purpose for *all* of their writing.

But more still needs to come out of the Writing Wednesday work in order to continually promote growth. Eventually, students need to know that at least some of their work will have a wider audience. Therefore, at the end of each instructional quarter, students will review the work contained in their Writer's Notebook and select one or more of their drafts to revise into a Publication Piece, an original creation that is shared with the broader class and graded. Although students will write far more drafts in their Writer's Notebook than they will revise, allowing students to select from their initial drafts reinforces the idea that all writing, even rough writing, serves a purpose. And because they will have already completed the hardest part—getting words on the page—and had an opportunity to get initial feedback from their Writing Team, students will be well-positioned to determine what revisions will help them strengthen their chosen draft. The revision stage of the journey occurs while students are preparing for the Celebration Days.

Celebration Days

Up until this point in the quarter, students' Writing Wednesday work has lived exclusively inside their Writer's Notebook. The majority of their work so far will be raw and incomplete—more of a promise than a realization of something great. It is important for students to have a space to produce this type of writing. We all know that in the real world, much of what we write ends up going nowhere. Perhaps we draft an email but, by the time we finish adjusting for tone and content, the majority of what we originally drafted is lost. Or perhaps we begin creating a resume but go through multiple drafts trying out a variety of layouts before we settle on the "right" version. As adults, we know that this process of drafting—and sometimes deleting—is not only normal but necessary to produce effective communication.

But we also know that some of our work *does* ultimately get published, that those drafts do eventually fuel something that is released to a larger audience. Just as asking students to write exclusively for Publication Pieces is unfair and unrealistic, so too is asking them to produce large quantities of drafts with no intention of developing them into something significant. If students feel that all of their Writing Wednesday work exists simply to live in their Writer's Notebooks, over time, they will lose any interest in continuing to write. And this is where Celebration Days come in.

Celebration Days provide an opportunity to balance the drafting and publishing stages. On any given Celebration Day, students come together both as individuals and as members of their Writing Team to showcase their best work and explore the best work of their fellow classmates. Each Celebration Day contains individual and group components and provides an opportunity for all students to have their voices heard and valued.

Planning for Celebration Days

Students will need time to plan for their Celebration Days. I recommend introducing students to the assignment instructions a few weeks before the end of the quarter and providing them with at least two ninety-minute (or four forty-five-minute) class periods for work time. During the first quarter, you may wish to introduce the assignment to students even earlier and provide additional work time to ensure they feel prepared for their first public sharing of their work.

Designing Celebration Day Activities

Celebration Day activities are a vital component of the Writing Wednesday process, but they can take a bit of advanced planning. To take some of the stress off teachers, particularly those who are integrating Writing Wednesdays for the first time, I have provided sample instructions to accompany each of the quarterly lesson sets. These instructions, however, assume that teachers have been moving through the book in sequence, and that certain lessons have been

completed in any given quarter. As such, if you make any deviations from the book, there is a possibility that the sample instructions may not align with the lessons you actually delivered. Therefore, teachers are strongly cautioned to review the lessons for each quarter and the accompanying Celebration Day instructions to determine what adjustments, if any, may be appropriate to make prior to assigning the Celebration Day assessment.

Remember, the activities in this book are designed with flexibility in mind. While it may sound great on paper to assume that a teacher can complete between four or five *Artfulness* lessons in any given quarter, as a teacher myself, I know that, in the real world, there are snow days and holidays, teacher workdays and assemblies. I know that some weeks will be better than others for integrating weekly writing and that teachers may not get to all of the lessons they hoped to teach in any given quarter. This book accounts for real-world considerations by providing lessons that are infinitely flexible, modifiable, and adaptable. With a little bit of advanced planning, you can easily ensure that all of your Writing Wednesday activities, including the culminating Celebration Day event, harmonize with your larger academic units and will still work even if scheduling conflicts create hurdles.

Buying snacks and drinks for each of your instructional blocks can get pricy. Ask your students if anyone is willing to bring snacks if permitted by your school.

Once you have determined what specific instructions to provide for your students, you should spend some time thinking about what your Celebration Day will actually look like. However you design them, I encourage you to consider making your Celebration Days an actual celebration. Place student desks together and spread tablecloths over them. Bring in snacks and drinks for them to enjoy as they explore their classmates' writing. Create a festive atmosphere that both takes the stress off of the performance part of the task and creates a sense of community among the participants. Later in the year, as students become more comfortable with sharing their writing, open the Celebration Days up to members of the larger school community by inviting guests to broaden students' audience.

Nuts-and-Bolts: Key Assumptions

Timing

As you begin planning for Writing Wednesdays, it's important to understand the key assumptions this book makes when developing the plans. Specifically, the lessons in this book assume:

- Ninety-minute instructional blocks that meet on alternating days (so that any given instructional block has a Writing Wednesday every other week, as opposed to each week)

- Four quarters per school year, with each quarter running approximately nine weeks

Based on the above, students in any given instructional block will have an opportunity to complete between four and five Writing Wednesdays per quarter. In practice, you may find that you are able to incorporate fewer Writing Wednesdays per quarter once interruptions for assemblies, holidays, and weather closures are factored in. While fewer Writing Wednesday lessons mean less practice for students, it will provide additional opportunities for you to select the lessons that will best fit your instructional needs at any given time.

If your instructional blocks are shorter than ninety minutes or if your classes meet every day rather than every other day, most lessons can easily be divided up into shorter increments and spread over multiple Wednesdays to complete. All lessons provide time suggestions for how long to spend on any given component, allowing for easy customization to suit your unique schedule.

Sequencing

This book organizes the Writing Wednesday activities by quarter, with each quarter targeting a range of academic skills. You can examine the lessons and key skills that are covered in any given quarter by exploring the "Look Inside" content provided on the opening pages of Chapters 2 through 5.

The sequence in which the lessons are introduced is meant only as a suggestion. Indeed, I often rearrange the order of the lessons to best suit our instructional needs. If you rearrange the sequence of the lessons, however, be sure to adjust your Celebration Day assignment instructions accordingly.

Student Population

Another key assumption made in this book concerns the age and skill of the students served. This book assumes that Writing Wednesday students will be in high school (9th-12th grade) and enrolled in an on-level ELA class. However, the lessons are designed with flexibility in mind and can easily be adjusted to support younger students, those in need of additional scaffolds, and accelerated learners. Each Writing Wednesday lesson provides suggestions on how to differentiate the lessons to either support or challenge learners as appropriate for your student population.

Additional Resources

To ensure you have the support you need as you integrate Writing Wednesdays into your own classes, *Artfulness* provides a variety of supplemental resources; some are embedded directly into the book and some can be accessed for free via the Members Only section of Alexandrite Publishing, LLC's website at www.alexandritepublishing.com.

Online resources directly connected to this book are organized by chapter for easy reference. In order to support a range of educational needs, additional instructional resources (not specifically aligned to this book) can also be found in the Members Only section of our website. New resources for teachers are added continually, so checking the website frequently will allow you to simplify your lesson planning throughout the year.

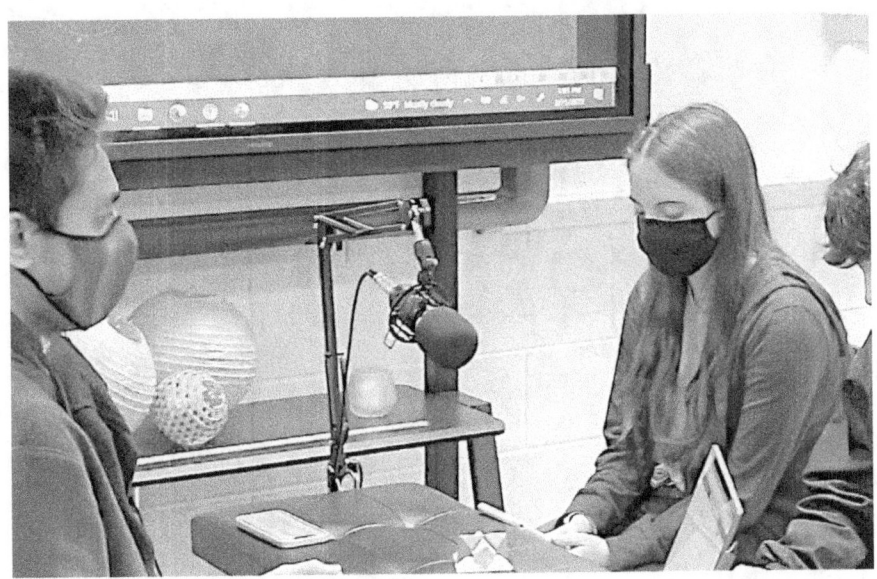

Figure 1.5 Celebration Day highlights.

2 Chapter

Look Inside Chapter 2

SCAN ME

Scan to access
supplemental
resources

Express Yourself
Prep Time: Medium

Description:

This lesson pairs famous portrait art with creative writing in order to inspire students to write personal narratives that reflect a unique and/or unexpected element of their identities. Students will begin by viewing a series of portrait art before considering their own unique identities and exploring ways to convey their unique identities in written form.

Student-Friendly Objectives:	*Materials:*
By the end of this lesson, students will be able to:	3-4 posters or large-scale color prints of unique portrait art, for example:
• Understand personal narratives as a form of both self-reflection and self-expression	• *At Eternity's Gate* by Vincent Van Gogh
	• *American Gothic* by Grant Wood
	• *The Two Fridas* by Frida Kahlo
• Explore identity in unconventional and unique ways	• *The Son of Man* by Rene Magritte
	• Graphic organizer to capture unique elements of students' identities

Rationale:

Each year, my students are asked to complete a personal narrative as part of an instructional unit. While some students take advantage of the opportunity to express themselves in meaningful ways, many of the personal narratives are almost indistinguishable from one another—there are no unique, unexpected details that differentiate one student from the next. Yet within the classroom, the various identities, perspectives, and personalities of my students are on full display. Clearly, there is a disconnect between who they are and how they see themselves. At a bare minimum, the consistent lack of originality present in many of their narratives reveals a hesitancy to take risks which is reinforced by lesson plans that move them through fill-in-the-blank style identity worksheets, yielding fairly similar results across the student population.

By beginning a personal narrative lesson instead with unexpected and unconventional approaches to portrait art, students come to see—literally—the power of a unique perspective. This inspiration serves as a launching point for them to take risks with their own writing by imagining themselves in ways that reflect who they are, what they struggle with, what they hope for. In this manner, this activity pushes the personal narrative genre in directions that many students are reluctant to initiate on their own and reassures them that there is no "one way" to see themselves. In addition to expanding their self-reflection skills, this lesson further advances the development of authentic, unique Writer's Voices.

Anticipatory Activity (20 minutes):

Before students enter the classroom, hang posters of your curated portrait art around the classroom. Once students are settled, ask them to take their Writer's Notebook around the room, stop at all of the gallery art on display, and review each portrait closely for at least two full minutes. Instructing students to mentally divide each portrait into quadrants will ensure full observation is made for each painting. Then, students should select at least two of the paintings to reflect upon in more detail. For each of their selected art pieces, students should jot down notes in the Observation section of their Writer's Notebook that include:

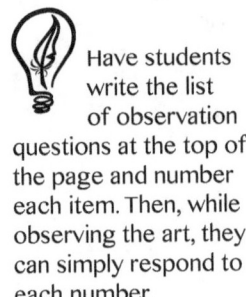

Have students write the list of observation questions at the top of the page and number each item. Then, while observing the art, they can simply respond to each number.

- The title of the art (this should be posted by the teacher next to each portrait)

- Their initial reaction to the art

- What they find unique, unconventional, or unexpected about the art

- What this art reveals or suggests about identity

- What specific details from the painting convey that revelation or suggestion

- What the viewer is left to infer about the subject of the painting

- Any other noteworthy observations or reflections

Once all students have had a chance to complete their notes, ask for volunteers to share brief observations and reflections about the art.

Artistic students often get bogged down in the details, struggling to make their sketches perfect. If this happens, remind students that this is a ten-minute "brainstorm" activity and their pace should reflect the purpose of this stage of the lesson.

Process (10 minutes):

Using their selected art as inspiration (note the word "inspiration" and not "template"), students should visualize an authentic, unique interpretation of themselves. Artistic students should be encouraged to complete a quick sketch of themselves. Students who are not inclined to sketch themselves literally should close their eyes to visualize what a self-portrait inspired by their chosen art might look like. Then, in their Writer's Notebook or using a graphic organizer like the one featured in **Figure 2.1** (see page 32), they should jot down the key details that will serve as inspiration for their personal narrative.

Drafting (50 minutes):

Now that they have a moment in their lives sketched out either visually or in outline format, students should spend the bulk of this class period drafting a narrative that captures that moment.

It is important to stress to students that they should not simply summarize what they see (i.e., they should not spend 50 minutes informing the reader that there is a person wearing a dark suit with an apple where his head should be). Rather, they should craft a *narrative* that conveys some larger idea behind how they see themselves. In other words, once students "see" themselves, they should decide if they want to take a self-reflective narrative approach that explores some internal tension, or a broader narrative approach that situates their identity within the context of the larger community.

Reflection (10 minutes):

Often, I ask students to share with their Writing Team before moving into the reflection stage. Since this activity is likely quite personal and their writing at this stage will probably be very rough, I recommend skipping the Team share today and asking students instead to move straight into the reflection stage. If students elect to continue working with this writing for a Publication Piece, they will have an opportunity to share with their Writing Team at that time.

For the reflection, ask students how the process of visualizing themselves in a moment in time shaped the way they conveyed their identity in writing.

- What unique or unexpected elements of their identity came to the forefront as part of this activity?

- How might they be able to use this new knowledge about themselves when crafting other, less personal, pieces of writing? For example, how might this activity affect their interpretation of perspective in broad terms, or how might they choose to experiment with voice or unique/unconventional literary elements in the future?

Differentiate

To Support:
This activity may challenge students in several ways. For struggling learners, it may be best to spend more time (perhaps the entire class period) creating a draft narrative connected directly to one of their chosen portraits rather than a self-reflection. Once they gain practice writing narratives (rather than summaries) of a visual text and feel confident with how to create and/or embed narrative elements into their writing, then they can move on to the personal narrative aspect of this activity (likely on a second instructional day).

Other students may struggle with the personal nature of this activity. If you suspect you have a number of students who may either struggle with 1) identifying something unique/unconventional about themselves; or 2) acknowledging/writing about something unique/unconventional about themselves, then consider dedicating one day to brainstorming, small-group chats, one-on-one conferences or other emotionally supportive activities and then using the information and support they gleaned from Day 1 to help them develop their drafts.

To Challenge:
Rather than crafting a personal narrative, ask students to mentally assemble each of the gallery-walk portraits from the anticipatory activity into a specific sequence that allows them to create one cohesive fictional narrative inspired by the full collection of portraits. The key to this challenge activity is to remind students that their narratives should be inspired by the portraits and should not simply summarize the portraits. This will allow greater creative flexibility. However, also remind students that they should be able to clearly point to support from the portraits themselves to justify their choices.

If you ask students to tackle this challenge activity, modify the reflection component so that students are asked to provide a detailed rationale for their choices which should explain the sequence of the inspiration portraits as well as information regarding where they incorporated details from each portrait into their writing either literally or in the abstract.

Figure 2.1 (From page 30)

Self-Portrait as Personal Narrative Pre-writing Brainstorm

STEP 1: Consider a moment, event, or feeling from your life. What are the most memorable, meaningful elements of that reflection? Use the space below to jot down your brainstorming. You may capture as many moments, events, or feelings as come to mind during this stage.

STEP 2: Now select one (1) of the moments, events, or feelings from your brainstorm list above. Using the details you connected to that memory, visualize the scene in the form of a self-portrait (along the lines of the images we explored in the anticipatory activity).

Environment: Are you . . .
- ☐ Alone
- ☐ With Others:
  - ○ 1
  - ○ 2
  - ○ 3 or more

Posture: Are you . . .
- ☐ Standing
- ☐ Sitting
- ☐ Running
- ☐ Walking
- ☐ Slouching
- ☐ Leaning
- ☐ Other: _____

Expression: Are you . . .
- ☐ Smiling
- ☐ Laughing
- ☐ Grinning
- ☐ Cringing
- ☐ Thinking
- ☐ Wondering
- ☐ Frowning
- ☐ Crying
- ☐ Other: _____

Setting: When you visualize yourself in this memory, where are you? For example, are you indoors or out? Are you in a realistic or abstract environment? What elements, if any, are in the background?

Symbolism: What objects, if any, are in the portrait with you and what is their significance to the reflection? What clothes are you wearing and how might your attire function to symbolically represent a key feature of your reflection?

Significance: What would you want your viewer to focus on in your self-portrait, and why? What do you want your viewer to learn about you, this moment, event, or feeling as a result of seeing the image?

STEP 3: Using the details captured above as inspiration, begin crafting a personal narrative that reflects the significance of this reflection. Employ narrative elements to show, in writing, your vision. Do not simply write a story that captures your responses to the questions above. Rather, use your responses above to develop a unique story that emphasizes an important part of your identity.

Suggested Unit Integration:
Embedding this activity into a larger reading unit of your choice will allow you to extract key passages from the whole-class reading, particularly those connected to characterization, and explore how the author's selection of detail helps create a vivid, unique portrayal. Pretty much any fictional text that occasionally veers into lengthier descriptions will frame this activity nicely. However, books that incorporate gothic, grotesque, and/or dystopian elements may work particularly well, as would books that are rich with irony, personification, and/or the unexpected.

Extension Activity:

- *Vocabulary:* Ask students to brainstorm a list of one or two words that connect meaningfully to each of the original anticipatory activity portraits. Then, ask students to present their words, definitions, and rationale for connecting each word to the original portrait. Once all students have argued for their words, have the class vote on which words should be selected as paired vocabulary and add them to an ongoing "Classroom Vocabulary" list.

- *Literary Analysis:* Link this activity either to a currently ongoing fiction unit or ask students to consider any number of texts you have already explored as a class. Then, ask them to match each of the anticipatory activity portraits with a corresponding character from their reading(s), providing a rationale to explain their choices:

    o What element of that character's life does this portrait seem to capture?

    o What textual evidence can students provide to support their claims?

- For an added challenge, turn this extension activity into a multimedia project where students pair the portrait with their

analytical findings in an organized, effective manner. Ask students to include quotes or passages from the text as part of their project (See **Figure 2.2** for sample instructions for this extension activity).

Figure 2.2

Extension Activity: Literary Analysis (Characterization)

Working Individually: Consider the characters in your novel carefully. Then, review and select any one of the portraits we explored in our Writing Wednesday activity, *Express Yourself,* that you feel connects meaningfully to one of the characters in your text. As part of your exploration, consider what specific elements of the paired portrait such as facial expressions, setting, tone, or mood seem to speak to your chosen character. Using your findings from this activity, write a literary analysis paragraph in which you argue how the author uses literary elements to develop that character and why this characterization is significant to our understanding of the larger narrative. Be sure to include specific textual evidence, complete with proper internal MLA citations, for support.

Working in Small Groups: As a group, consider the characters in your novel carefully. Then, match all four of the portraits we explored in our Writing Wednesday activity, *Express Yourself,* with corresponding characters from your text (you can select from both major and minor characters). As a group, seek out textual evidence to support each of your pairings, being careful to consider how each portrait reflects the characterization from the novel. Finally, create a multimedia project in which you present your findings to the class, being sure to incorporate both visual and written components (including quoted evidence) into your product. Attach a properly formatted Works Cited page to reflect your references to the novel and each of the portraits.

- *Persuasion:* Ask Writing Teams to brainstorm products, ideas, or services that are connected to one or more of the anticipatory activity portraits. Then, ask them to use that portrait as a visual foundation for a persuasive poster in order to practice persuasive appeals in advertising.

- *Research/Nonfiction:* Ask students to research one of the artists from the anticipatory activity portrait collection and create a mini research project that explores some element of the artist's life or his/her work. For example, students may be asked to research and present a brief biography of the artist's life, other works, and how this particular portrait fits into the larger volume of that artist's work.

Conventions of Genre
Prep Time: Medium

Description:

In this writing lesson, students will experiment writing in a variety of genres in order to gain an understanding of how form and genre shape meaning. Students will first work with the writing of others by converting, for example, a piece of prose writing into another genre such as poetry or drama. Then, they will work with their own authentic writing sample to convert their draft into two or more different genres. The lesson will end with a reflection that asks students to thoughtfully consider the impact of form and genre on an author's message.

Student-Friendly Objectives:	*Materials:*
By the end of this lesson, students will be able to: <ul><li>Recognize the conventions of two or more literary genres</li><li>Understand the effect of form and genre on author's purpose and message</li></ul>	<ul><li>Copies of selected mentor texts</li><li>*Optional*: Graphic organizer for students to work with while exploring the mentor texts</li></ul>

Rationale:

As teachers, we often incorporate some degree of genre study into our ELA curriculum. We may, for example, include some nonfiction articles or paired poetry within the context of a larger narrative unit of study. However, we often fail to explore the *effect* of form and genre on the way a message is delivered and received. By asking students to write and rewrite the same text into two or more genres, students come face-to-face with the consequences of selecting one form and genre over another. As they grapple with which details from the original narrative to include, revise, or rearrange, they come to understand the options they have as writers and how the choices authors make in connection to those options shape the reader's perception of a text.

Freewrite (5 minutes):

Provide students with a prompt of your choice. For example, you may provide them with a craft-focused prompt that asks them to develop a character narrative, a reflective prompt that asks them to explore some element of their own identities, or a thematic prompt that asks them to develop a piece of writing based upon an idea or concept. Then, have students spend five minutes writing to the prompt in their Writer's Notebook, making sure that they continue writing for the full five minutes.

Process (30 minutes):

Provide students with a set of short mentor texts in a variety of genres. Since this is a one-day activity, be sure to consider pacing when determining how to design your lesson. The table in **Figure 2.3** provides some suggested options when selecting your mentor texts for this activity.

Figure 2.3
Selecting Mentor Texts Based on Instructional Goals

Emphasis on Poetry	Contrast a series of extremely short poems such as haikus or epigrams against longer poems such as odes or sonnets. By selecting a variety of different poetic forms that speak to a common theme or focus, students will consider the relationship between form and meaning.
Emphasis on Shorter Prose	Select a variety of vignettes, extremely short fiction, six-word memoirs, and/or short stories in order to explore how length affects meaning. Students will explore what happens to word choice and syntax when authors are constrained to a couple of lines and the difference between a vignette and an extremely short story. This approach will also cause them to consider how narrative prose affects elaboration and the development of ideas.
Emphasis on Multiple Genres	Mix and match from the list above (or supplement additional genres such as visual art, graphic novels, and advertisements as desired). Providing a variety of texts will allow students to compare and contrast how a multitude of forms and genres affects meaning. To make this approach effective, be sure to control the variables by selecting mentor texts that share a common theme or focus. In this manner, students can isolate the impact of form—as opposed to content—on the development of the author's purpose and message.

As an alternative, incorporating this activity into a larger unit on fiction and genre will allow you to explore mentor texts in advance of this lesson, leaving more time for students to experiment with drafting today. **Figure 2.4** provides some options for how to integrate mentor texts in a way that targets specific learning objectives.

Figure 2.4	Integrating the Mentor Texts
Exploring Individually	Place mentor texts at various stations around the room. Individually, students circulate to each station, taking notes about the conventions and techniques associated with each genre in the Observation section of their Writer's Notebook. When they return to their seats, students spend five minutes reflecting on how the various conventions and techniques they observed affected their understanding of the text.
Exploring in Teams	Provide each Writing Team a set of mentor texts. Once each Team member has had an opportunity to read each text, students work together to discuss the specific conventions and techniques of each genre and the effect of those conventions and techniques on meaning.

Drafting (45 minutes):
Students revise their freewrite prompt to fit two or more of the genres explored in today's lesson.

o *First* (5 minutes): Students review their notes to consider the various mentor texts they explored. Based on their original freewrite draft and their personal preferences from the genre study, students will select at least two of the genres explored during the mentor text activity to attempt during the revision stage.

o *Second* (20 minutes): Using their first choice of mentor text as a guide, students should consider the conventions of their selected genre. They should then annotate their original freewrite to determine which elements from the original draft to include into the new genre, which elements to rearrange,

which elements to revise, and which elements to omit in order to align with the conventions of that genre. Then, students should spend the remainder of their twenty minutes revising their freewrite to reflect their findings.

o *Third* (20 minutes): Using their second choice of mentor text as a guide, students should repeat the process outlined above, this time to align their draft with the conventions of the second genre.

Reflection (10 minutes): Students spend the final ten minutes of class reflecting in their Writer's Notebook upon their genre exploration.

- What observations did they make about how length, form, and genre affected meaning?

- What did they have to change when they revised their own writing in order to fit each respective genre?

- What are the advantages and disadvantages of each form?

- How do the differences between the genres shape the choices a writer makes and the way a reader may come to understand the text?

- How can they use this new understanding to help them in the development of their own original writing in the future?

Differentiate

To Support:

Divide this lesson into two instructional days. On Day 1, focus on the mentor texts, providing students more time to explore and observe each text. At the end of the mentor text exploration, bring students together in their Teams to discuss their observations, paying particular attention to an exploration of how the various forms and genres affected the author's message. Teams then share their observations with the class, comparing and contrasting the responses across groups to deepen their understanding.

On Day 2, students spend the bulk of their time revising their original freewrite to fit each genre. You may wish to review the previous day's lesson (particularly if you have a break of a week or more in between writing days) before they begin the writing process. Students will write for 60 minutes before moving into their Writing Teams where they will spend the remaining 30 minutes sharing out both versions of their text. Teams will close out the day by considering how each genre affected both the development of ideas and the stylistic choices of the author.

To Challenge:

- *Extend*: Ask advanced writers to take their favorite version of their draft through the full writing process in order to be developed into a Publication Piece. Along with their final submission, they should be asked to reflect on what they learned about genre through this process including, specifically, an exploration of how length, form, and genre shapes meaning. They should refer to specific elements of their writing to justify their findings.

- *Double-Extend*: Have gifted or advanced students apply their new understanding of genre to an analysis of a whole-class text being studied in the broader instructional unit. The analysis task should require students to focus their arguments on an exploration of how genre affects meaning.

Suggested Unit Integration:

This lesson can be easily incorporated into any number of curriculum units of study. Depending on your classroom needs, you can include this activity at the beginning of the year to explore genre in the broadest terms, in a poetry unit where you are exploring a variety of poetic forms, or in a narrative prose unit where you are exploring elements such as diction, syntax, elaboration, selection of details, and

development of ideas. This activity can also easily serve as an end-of-year review of the various genres they have studied. If you choose to incorporate this activity into one or more of your larger curriculum units, use your time on instructional (i.e., non-writing) days to explore each mentor text in detail, focusing on the unique characteristics of each genre. Then, reclaim the mentor text time from the original lesson plan for students to engage more fully with the drafting stage of the process, conference with the teacher, or work in their Writing Teams.

Extension Activities:

Skip ahead to **Figure 2.12** to see sample instructions for a year-long Technical Vocabulary project.

- *Vocabulary:* Ask students to keep a Technical Vocabulary list of the different writing genres you explore over the course of the school year. For each genre, students should identify the definition, key hallmarks of that genre, authors who are known for that genre, and one or two short samples that showcase that genre.

- *Literary Analysis:* Provide students with two short fiction texts that share a common theme but utilize different writing genres. Then, ask students to compare and contrast the development of the theme through the author's use of genre, producing a short literary analysis argument that explores how genre shapes meaning.

- *Writer's Portfolio:* To extend the lesson further, ask students to continually add to their genre study by developing a portfolio of writing samples across a wide range of genres. This option will likely work best as a year-long exercise, with students adding to their portfolio as they move through the units. At the end of the portfolio project, students should review and reflect upon their learning, highlighting, for example, areas of growth, areas of success, and areas of joy. As part of the portfolio task, students should reflect upon how writing across genres has informed their understanding of the writing process and, more specifically, the role that authorial choice plays in developing ideas and shaping understanding. See **Figure 2.5** for sample instruction language for this extension activity.

Figure 2.5

Extension Activity: Genre Portfolio

Directions: Over the course of the school year, you will encounter numerous texts across a variety of genres. As you explore different styles of writing, you will maintain a portfolio in which you track the different genres and their conventions. By the end of the year, you will produce a Summative Genre Portfolio project that showcases your selected genres from the list below.

Prose Texts:

Full-Length Novel	Short Story	Vignette
Extremely Short Fiction	Dramatic Script	Narrative Blog

Visual Texts:

Photo Essay	Visual Social Media	Documentary/Film

Nonfiction Texts:

Narrative Nonfiction	Social Media	Podcast
News Article	Listicle	Nonfiction Blog

Poetic Texts:

Ode	Sonnet	Ekphrastic Poem
Free Verse	Narrative Poem	Documentary Poem
Pastoral Poem	Haiku	Ballad

Requirements: Your portfolio must include at least five (5) different genres including:

- ❏ One prose text
- ❏ One visual text
- ❏ One nonfiction text
- ❏ One poetic text
- ❏ Student choice (from list above)

Portfolio:

For each of your selected genres, your portfolio should include the following:

- ❏ Name of selected genre
- ❏ Title/author of exemplar text
- ❏ For shorter pieces, a copy of the complete exemplar text. For longer pieces, a key excerpt. If print copies of the text are not available or feasible, include a link to access a digital version of the text.
- ❏ Key conventions of that genre and examples of where those conventions can be found in your selected text.
- ❏ An original piece crafted by you in which you showcase the key conventions of that genre
- ❏ A reflection that considers how exploring and writing across genres has informed your understanding of the writing process and, more specifically, the role that authorial choice plays in developing ideas and shaping understanding. You must cite specific examples from your portfolio to support your findings.
- ❏ A properly formatted Works Cited page for each of the exemplar texts included in your portfolio

Artfulness

Rolling the Dice
Prep Time: Low

Description:

This lesson incorporates games of chance into the creative writing process. While students spend the majority of today's class engaged in creative writing tasks, the requirements for the day's activities will be left to chance. In this activity, students will roll the dice to determine the number of each required story element they must include. For example, if the story element being played is "character" and the student rolls a 3, the student will be forced to incorporate three unique characters into their narrative. The teacher can adjust this game to incorporate as few or as many chance elements as desired, so this game could be played repeatedly throughout the year by simply increasing the challenge level students face each time.

Student-Friendly Objectives: By the end of this lesson, students will be able to: • Plan and organize their writing for a variety of purposes • Effectively incorporate literary elements into their own writing	*Materials:* • Dice • Literary Element Prompts • Playing Cards

Rationale:

Although this activity provides students with nearly unlimited writing choices, the forced elements require them to engage in critical thinking as they must carefully consider how and where to insert their required components. The more forced elements they are required to include —and the more suddenly they are asked to include them—the more critical thinking and revision they will need to do. This activity, therefore, not only requires students to thoughtfully consider how multiple literary elements connect to one another to develop a cohesive narrative, but also requires them to adjust their writing to address specific writing goals.

Rolling the Dice (10 minutes):

As students enter the classroom, ask them to identify and call out as many literary elements as they can (for example, character, internal conflict, etc.). Write these elements on the board. Then, assign each of these elements a corresponding playing card number (1–10 or, if they have identified more than 10, include face cards as well).

Roll the dice to see how many playing cards will be pulled. This will represent the number of different literary elements students incorporate into their own creative writing pieces.

Fan the cards out and ask students at random to pull one of the cards (if you rolled a 4, for example, ask four different students to pull cards). Match the number on the card to the corresponding literary element. These will be the literary elements students will be required to insert into their writing.

For each literary element you pulled, roll the dice once more (or have a student selected at random roll the dice). The number rolled determines the quantity of that element they have to incorporate into their writing. For example, if they roll a 2 and the literary element is setting, they must include two different settings into their narrative. Repeat this process for each required literary element. See **Figure 2.6** for more detailed instructions.

Drafting (60 minutes):

Students will spend sixty minutes drafting today. To keep them writing for the full sixty minutes, I recommend providing them with specific requirements for each literary element (e.g., developing a character who just moved to the area or incorporating a grocery store as one of their required settings) and then staggering when you ask students to insert the required elements. For example, if they pulled three characters, you may get them started with one character description, and then, about fifteen minutes into their drafting time, provide them with a second character description they need to incorporate.

This activity doubles nicely as an informative assessment. When students call out various literary elements, you can quickly determine both which terms they are most familiar with and which terms they may need to be taught or retaught. If you find that students are calling out sophisticated literary elements, that may indicate that you can breeze past review and reteaching of lower-level core skills.

If this lesson is completed at multiple points during the year, you can use it to help you assess students' evolving understanding of literary elements over time as well.

Figure 2.6

Rolling the Dice Process

STEP 1: Ask students to call out as many literary elements as they can think of (character, metaphor, setting, chronological sequence, etc.). Then, assign each of the elements they identify a number 1–13 (If they call out more than thirteen literary elements, remove the ones that would be too difficult for their skill level).

Example:

1. Character	5. Symbol
2. Setting	6. Repetition
3. Internal Conflict	7. Non-linear Structure
4. External Conflict	8. Foreshadowing

STEP 2: Roll the Dice. This will determine how many literary elements to incorporate.

 Example: You roll a 4—students will be asked to incorporate four different literary elements from the student-generated list into their narrative.

STEP 3: After assigning a number to each of the literary elements identified, open a  card deck and pull out one of each of the corresponding number and face cards, as applicable (for example, the six card would align with repetition from the list above.) Then, ask four different students to pull one card each from that stack.

Example: Students pull an ace, a 3, a 6, and a 7. Using the list from Step 1 above, they will be required to incorporate character, internal conflict, repetition, and non-linear structure into their original narrative.

 **STEP 4:** Now that the literary elements have been chosen, students will roll the dice again to determine how many of each required element students will need to incorporate. Using the example above, ask four different students to roll the dice. Each roll will determine the number of characters, internal conflict, and repetition they will need to incorporate (if students pull a structural element like linear/non-linear organization, no roll is required since the text's organization will need to be woven throughout their piece).

Writing Team Share (20 minutes):
Writing Teams will spend the final twenty minutes of class reading their stories to each other, exploring where and how each student incorporated the required elements into their narratives. Because of the impromptu nature of this activity, they will not be asked to discuss or reflect upon their strategy while writing. Instead, they'll simply have fun and enjoy their unexpected creations.

Differentiate

To Support:
To support younger/struggling learners, minimize the number of required story elements and/or keep the integration criteria broad. For example, if they are required to incorporate two literary conflicts, allow them to select their own conflicts rather than providing them a description such as "woman running late for the bus." Alternatively, provide students with three or four specific options for students to select from for their required element. In the previous example, students may be permitted to choose: "woman running late for the bus" or "man who stepped in gum" or "child who lost their jacket." Allow students to work individually or in pairs so they can choose how much or how little support they would like for this activity.

To Challenge:
The most effective way to increase the rigor of this activity is to require more literary elements and/or more complex, narrow, or specific literary elements. For example, I once required students to integrate "I forgot my turkey sandwich" into their stories! The greater the number and the more specific the requirements, the more difficult the challenge.

Suggested Unit Integration:

Embed this activity in any close reading unit you are conducting with your students. Provide students with a lengthy passage (one or two typed pages) from a whole-class reading and ask them to highlight all the different literary elements they see in the passage using a different color for each literary element they find. Then, ask them to mark how many different types of each literary element are present in that passage. Finally, ask them to consider how the author uses literary elements to shape meaning. Consider completing a before-and-after version of this activity to assess students' growth with close reading and analysis skills.

Artfulness

Simply have students complete the above activity both before and after engaging in today's lesson, using a different, but structurally similar, passage to work with during the "after" stage. Then, either compare their growth as part of a formative assessment or ask students to review and reflect upon their own growth, noting their observations in their Writer's Notebook so they can track their learning over the course of the year.

Earlier in the year, consider limiting the number of literary elements you ask students to explore and integrate. Later in the year, increase the challenge by exploring a wider range of literary elements both within your instructional units and for the *Rolling the Dice* activity.

Extension Activity:

- *Literary Analysis:* Working with a whole-class reading, ask students to explore a lengthy passage of the text or the text as a whole and then write a literary analysis essay that explores how the author uses literary elements to shape meaning. Challenge students to avoid the three-pronged thesis which would likely result in students exploring each literary element used by the author in isolation. Rather, ask them to develop a cohesive, unified argument that explores how the author develops the narrative using layers of literary elements in order to shape the meaning of the work as a whole.

- *Revision Process—Self Reflection:* Ask students to select one of their previous drafts in their Writer's Notebook and integrate x number of new literary elements into that writing. Then, conduct a compare/contrast analysis to explore how the story changed with the addition of these devices. Which version did they like best and why? What have they learned about the writing process as a result of that activity? See **Figure 2.7** for sample instructions for this extension activity.

- *Vocabulary:* Ask students to consider what they have learned about literary elements as a result of this activity and then revisit their definitions and/or examples of literary elements in their Technical Vocabulary list to capture this new understanding. For example, how might they update their understanding of "characterization" after having pulled a character prompt that requires them to integrate someone who is obsessed with goldfish? How might they approach the crafting of fictional characters in the future now that they have explored such a narrow example of character?

Figure 2.7

Extension Activity: Revision & Self-Reflection

Directions: Now that you have learned how to consider and integrate a variety of literary elements into your writing, review your earlier Writing Wednesday drafts and select one that would benefit from revision. Using the list of required elements from our *Rolling the Dice* activity, annotate your earlier draft to determine where and how to incorporate these new elements. Also consider ways to improve upon the literary elements already included in your draft. Remember to consider your purpose—what idea or message are you trying to explore in your narrative and how will your incorporation of these elements help you achieve and enhance your goal?

Then, begin revising your draft based on your notes. Once you have completed your revision, add a reflection below your update in which you:

➤ Compare and contrast the original to the revised version to explore how the overall narrative evolved as a result of your changes

➤ Consider which version you liked best and why, and

➤ Reflect upon what you have learned about literary elements and the writing process generally as a result of this activity.

Story Swap
Prep Time: Low

Description:

In this activity, students gain practice in adjusting their writing to fit different purposes. Students begin with a story prompt that requires them to create a story recipe, essentially an outline of what their story will be. Before they start drafting, however, they are forced to swap story recipes with a neighbor and then must write their neighbor's brainstormed story instead.

At a designated point in the drafting stage, they will be required to swap stories with the same neighbor again so that their original narrative idea is returned to them. They must spend the remainder of the block familiarizing themselves with their neighbor's version of their story and then continuing the story so that it forms one cohesive narrative.

Student-Friendly Objectives:
By the end of this lesson, students will be able to:

- Brainstorm and organize ideas for writing
- Adapt writing to fit different purposes

Materials:

- Story starting prompt(s)
- Story Recipe Graphic Organizer

Rationale:

Although this activity provides tons of creative options for students to express themselves, the swap element forces them to engage in critical thinking and revision while drafting. As a result, students learn how to adjust their writing—and their plans for writing—to meet new contexts. This activity incorporates close reading, critical thinking, revision, collaboration, and allows students to simultaneously develop and share their writing with a classmate in order to enhance their writing skills.

Anticipatory Activity (15 minutes):
Briefly review writing outlines as a pre-writing tool, sharing examples and discussing how they function as appropriate. Then discuss the idea of story recipes which are, essentially, rough outlines (see **Figure 2.8** for a sample story recipe template). Tell students that they will be practicing their pre-writing skills by developing a story recipe in conjunction with their writing prompt for the day.

Next, assign the writing prompt that students will be working with. Be specific enough that they have a clear direction in which to head. For example: character with a limp, night, lost wallet.

Provide a few minutes for students to develop their story recipes based on their prompt.

Recipe Swap (5 minutes):
Once students have their story recipes created but before they begin drafting, ask students to swap their story recipes (and their prompt if unique to each student) with a neighbor. Once they have swapped recipes, students will need to carefully review the prompt and their new recipe card as they will spend their writing time developing their neighbor's story. Students should not ask their neighbor any questions. They should simply work with the recipe, the prompt, and go from there.

Drafting (20 minutes):
Students will spend the next twenty minutes drafting their narrative using their neighbor's prompt and story recipe as their guide.

Story Swap (5 minutes):
After twenty minutes of drafting time, have students swap stories again with the same partner. At this point, they should have their own original prompt and story recipe but their neighbor's draft of that story. They should spend a few minutes reading over their neighbor's work to get a sense of the story that was being created before they continue that story.

Artfulness

Figure 2.8

Story Recipe Card

Setting(s): _____

Character(s): _____

Internal Conflict(s): _____

External Conflict(s): _____

Narration:

- ❑ First
- ❑ Second
- ❑ Third Limited
- ❑ Third Omniscient

Organizational Structure:

- ❑ Linear
- ❑ Circular
- ❑ Parallel
- ❑ Fractured

Format (choose one):

- ❑ Short Story
- ❑ Poem
- ❑ Journal/Diary Entry
- ❑ News Article
- ❑ Blog
- ❑ Musical Album
- ❑ Other: _____

Genre: (choose one):

- ❑ Drama
- ❑ Comedy
- ❑ Horror/Gothic
- ❑ Action/Adventure
- ❑ Historical Fiction
- ❑ Nonfiction
- ❑ Other: _____

Brainstorm:

Drafting (20 minutes):
Students spend the next twenty minutes continuing the narrative, challenging themselves to develop their portion so that the ideas flow logically and cohesively with what came before. In other words, the final story should feel like one unified story rather than two different stories tied together.

Writing Team Share (20 minutes):
Students now assemble into pairs of Writing Teams (i.e., two different Writing Teams will work together). Each student from one Team will read their narrative aloud exactly as written. The other Writing Team will score each narrative on a 1–5 scale with 1 representing the least cohesion and 5 representing the most cohesion. The student with the highest cohesion score will "win" this activity. The process then repeats so that the other Team has the opportunity to share and have their work evaluated.

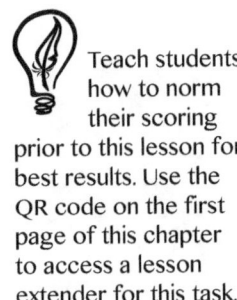 Teach students how to norm their scoring prior to this lesson for best results. Use the QR code on the first page of this chapter to access a lesson extender for this task.

Reflection (5 minutes):
Students will spend five minutes reflecting in their Writer's Notebook about this process.

- How comfortable did they feel with the pre-writing process of creating a story recipe?

- How useful was the story recipe when trying to develop their neighbor's story?

- What strategies did they have to employ to blend two different visions for the same narrative into one cohesive text?

- How successful did they feel and why?

Differentiate

To Support:	To Challenge:
Support younger/struggling students by adjusting the "ingredients" listed in the story recipe organizer to best reflect the story structures they are most familiar with and consider reducing the number of elements they can select from to avoid overwhelming them with choices. When it comes time for the second swap—when the stories have already entered the drafting stage—consider having partners work together to select the story they think is most workable as a team effort and then have them work together on one cohesive narrative, rather than individually on two separate narratives.	Increase the challenge by requiring that additional story elements be integrated into the writing during both drafting stages. For example, during the first round of drafting, require a particular character type to be added effectively into the narrative, and during the second round of drafting, require a new setting, conflict, or dialogue element be added. Adjust the challenge of the required elements up or down to increase the rigor as appropriate for your classes.

Suggested Unit Integration:

Embed this activity in a larger lesson on the writing process. Because this lesson targets pre-writing strategies (brainstorming, outlining), this is a good lesson to incorporate earlier in the school year in connection with any lesson that addresses the writing process. This works as a great hands-on activity when teaching students how to plan their writing to target particular purposes and audiences, and also provides tools and strategies students can use when planning and organizing their writing. The story-swap component of this lesson targets the revision process and would work well either at the beginning of the year in anticipation of later revision assessments, or later in the year to measure progress and growth with revision skills.

Extension Activity:

- *Fan Fiction:* Ask students to demonstrate their skill as collaborative Writers by selecting one of their favorite texts and using a literary element from that story (for example, a character, a setting, a conflict) as inspiration for their own original fan fiction (see **Figure 2.9** for sample instructions for this extension activity). Extend the learning further by layering in persuasive writing skills by asking students to include a text description to accompany their creation with the goal of persuading others to read their work.

Figure 2.9

Extension Activity: Fan Fiction

Fan Fiction!

Congratulations on having successfully demonstrated that you can work with the writing of others to create an original narrative of your own. Now it's time to show off your creation skills and celebrate your favorite author or story by developing your own original fan fiction!

Select a story from a text you love and identify a character, a setting, or an event from that story that will serve as the inspiration for your paired piece. You must incorporate sufficient elements from the original story to keep the connection solid, but remember, this is your writing, so there should be plenty of original content as well.

Once you have drafted and revised your piece to your satisfaction, be sure to include a detailed reflection as part of your submission. Your reflection should include:

➢ The title and author of your inspiration piece

➢ What literary element(s) you took inspiration from

➢ What elements from the original narrative you incorporated into your own piece

➢ Why you made the choices you did and what overall effect you were hoping to achieve

Remember to include specific, quoted references from both the source material and your original narrative to support your rationale.

- *Literary Analysis:* Embed this activity in a whole-class reading unit. After students have completed this activity, ask them to demonstrate their understanding of authorial choice by exploring how their text's author uses literary elements (whichever elements you featured in your story recipe activity) to shape meaning.

Artfulness

- *Publication Piece—Co-authors:* Ask writing partners to develop this piece into a polished Publication Piece but with a catch— they must work together to co-author the story. This not only targets collaborative learning skills, but it forces students to carefully consider and adapt two unique voices and styles so that the finished piece feels cohesive and unified. As a result, the writing partners will need to take this piece through multiple rounds of revision, enhancing their understanding of the writing process. In addition, to make the piece feel seamless, they will need to develop an understanding of—and a control over—the idea of a Writer's Voice.

The Genre Challenge
Prep Time: High

Description:

In this lesson, students explore how genre shapes characterization in fiction texts. Students will read a short narrative that is rich with characterization details. This narrative can be an excerpt from a longer piece of narrative fiction, or a complete short narrative in the form of a vignette, a poem, an extremely short story, etc. The key is to ensure that whatever narrative you select, the character (or speaker, if a poem) has a strong presence. Students explore and evaluate what details in the text develop this character and then create a character sketch based on the original text. They then place this character in a new genre. For example, if the character was discovered occupying the space of a longer piece of fiction, they imagine what might happen to this character if they were relocated to a poem, or an extremely short story. Finally, students reflect upon the impact of genre on characterization in order to better understand the art of creative writing. **Figure 2.10** provides some elements to consider as you customize this lesson for your own classes.

Figure 2.10

As you decide how to implement this activity, consider expanding your definition of "genre" beyond short stories, poems, and the like in order to capture a wide-range of writing that reflects students' lived experiences. Examples of authentic genres might include sitcoms, song lyrics, performance videos, online profiles, blogs, brochures, podcasts, and more.

Also, take care to design this lesson in a way that reflects a variety of voices and perspectives. For example:

- Provide different Writing Teams with different excerpts and/or source characters. If you choose this path, selecting a wide variety of genres and characters which showcase distinct voices will provide a variety of perspectives.

- Ask students to relocate the source character into a genre that is significantly different from the source text. If the source text, for example, pulls from a pre-nineteenth century English novel, perhaps this character (the traits, not the actual character) can be relocated to a 1990s sitcom, a dating profile, or a performance video. What elements of that character get highlighted or minimized in the new genre? How does the character's voice change? etc.

*Artfulness*

Student-Friendly Objectives:	*Materials:*
By the end of this lesson, students will be able to:	• Class-set of the inspiration text(s) to explore characterization
• Recognize the role of genre on the development of character	
• Understand how genre affects meaning	

Rationale:

When we teach students to explore literature, we often ask them to consider the *effect* of the choices an author makes on meaning. However, students often struggle with both components of this question: 1) what do we mean by "effect" and how is the effect determined (the most common response I see in my ELA classrooms across all levels of instruction, for example, is that the author made x choice in order to make the story more realistic . . .), and 2) what choices are we exploring? We can often clarify the second portion of their confusion relatively easily by, for example, giving them a focus for reading (we are exploring characterization today, or we are exploring the author's use of irony). However, regardless of how we narrow down the focus, the response is almost always the same: "The author made x choice in order to make the story more realistic." Thus, we end up exactly where we started out before we clarified the question.

Incorporating creative writing tasks that explore discrete choices by asking the students to manipulate those choices in their own writing helps students conceptualize the concept of "authorial choice" and "effect" in ways that discussions alone often don't. Students themselves, when writing reflections for creative tasks, often discuss how challenging they found the activity because they had to force their own creative ideas into a set structure. The confines of the literary element being explored—be it genre, figurative devices, conflict, or form—force students to grapple with the construction of their texts in ways that formulaic writing tasks do not. Suddenly they have to think about word choice, syntax, organization and more in ways they rarely do when they plug and drop writing components into prescribed templates.

This creative writing task, therefore, leads students to a deeper and more meaningful understanding of the role of choice—in this case, the choice of genre—in shaping a narrative. Because they are working with a control element (character), they can see what happens to characterization when genre shifts, thus opening up their understanding of "effect" beyond the limits of "because it makes it more realistic." This experience then shapes their own understanding of craft in future literary analysis pieces by providing them with a better understanding of the role of choice on meaning.

Anticipatory Activity (15 minutes):
Provide students with a short source text in which they will meet their character. During the first five minutes of class, students simply read the mentor text, annotating where appropriate as they do a quick exploration of character.

Character Mapping (20 minutes):
During the next twenty minutes, students work either alone or in Teams (at the teacher's discretion) to map their character. Although this can be done in a very straightforward manner (what do we learn about the character and what textual evidence supports our findings?), this can also provide a great opportunity to extend learning and/or integrate play. Here are some examples, each of which requires textual evidence for support:

- *To Include Interview Skills:* In the class periods leading up to today's lesson, provide students with a *brief* description of a character (or set of characters, to increase the challenge). For example: name, occupation, age. Ask students to develop a set of interview questions that may help reveal more about this character and then set those interview questions aside. On the day of this lesson, after students have read the provided source text, they must strive to answer those questions, using textual evidence to support their responses.

- *To Promote Collaboration:* Adapt this activity even further by placing students in pairs. One student takes on the persona of the character from the source text. The other acts as the interviewer.

Artfulness

The interviewer asks the questions and the other student, in the persona of the character, must answer the questions. At the end of the activity, the partners will have a character map based on the questions they developed (see **Figure 2.11** for sample instructions for the Interview task).

Figure 2.11

Character Interview

NOTE TO TEACHER: Working with the class text(s), develop a brief character sketch (age, occupation, time period, etc.) for the characters in the story. These will be given to students during Step 1 below (1 per student). In Step 2, students will receive the name of a different character from the story. Pair students up so that one student will have received the character sketch of the character name that the other student was assigned to closely explore during reading).

STEP 1 (Pre-Reading): Using the character sketch you were given, generate at least ten (10) quality interview questions that will allow you to learn more about this character in upcoming lessons. Arrive at class on (INSERT DATE) with your questions ready.

STEP 2 (During Reading): Closely read your text to track the character you were assigned. As you do, keep a reading log to capture any key quotes, along with corresponding page numbers, that help develop this character and the reader's understanding of them. Be sure to write down your reflections about the significance of your observations as well. You will bring your notes with you (along with your Interview Questions from Step 1 above) to class on (INSERT DATE).

STEP 3: Working with your partner, take turns playing the "Interviewer" or the "Character" based on the character sketches and characters you were assigned.

❖ The Interviewer should ask the questions developed in Step 1 and write the responses – along with the location of supporting source material – on the Interview Form.

❖ The Character should take on the persona of their assigned character in order to answer the interview questions to the best of their ability. Use the notes taken in Step 2 to inform the responses, being sure to provide the Interviewer with page numbers when available to support your responses.

By the end of Step 3, you and your partner should have a detailed understanding of two of the characters from your text. You will each then select one (1) of the characters, along with your findings, to complete the Genre Challenge.

- *To Incorporate Visual Media:* Post pictures and/or paintings of people around the room in various situations, environments, and with various expressions. After students read the source text, they walk around the room to find the visual portrayal that best fits their character. They must develop a character sketch of their character by considering both the original source text and the elements of the portrayal they feel best matches that character, being sure to justify their choices with textual evidence.

Drafting (50 minutes):
Determine whether students will be working individually, with partners, or in Writing Teams (or if you want to allow students to choose how to work). Then, provide students with fifty minutes to relocate their characters into their new genre. Some options for determining which genre they will be writing in include:

- *Teacher Choice:* The most straight-forward option, in this version, the teacher determines which genre students will work with. This option is great for novice learners (students who are only familiar with a small handful of genres) or times when the teacher wants to focus on the conventions of one particular genre as part of a larger unit (e.g., drama, poetry, persuasion).

- *Student Choice:* Allow students to select which new genre to drop their character into. Be sure to provide a wide variety of possible genres including, for example, vignettes, short story, extremely short fiction, poetry, music lyrics, podcasts, television interview or sitcom, poster, online profile, blog, dramatic scene, etc. This option works best if students are already familiar with each of the genre options. If they are unfamiliar with the genre, they may spend more time trying to understand that genre than writing.

- *A Game of Chance:* Have students play a game to determine their new genre. This could be as simple as pulling a genre from a hat or can be more playful—a spinning wheel, an indoor bowling game, matching a dice roll to a genre, etc.

- *Musical Chairs:* Place different genres face-down on each student desk (or in stations, if students are working in Teams). Have students move around the room while music is playing. When the music stops, they sit at whichever desk is closest to them and the genre that is posted on their desk is the genre they will be writing.

Once the genre has been determined, students will spend the balance of the fifty minutes drafting.

Reflection (5 minutes):
In the final few minutes of class, students reflect upon this activity, focusing specifically on how the change in genre affected the presentation of character.

- What details of the character came into focus when the genre changed?
- What details were minimized?
- How did genre affect the character's voice and other outward traits?
- How did the genre impact what inward traits were emphasized or hidden?
- In what way(s) does genre shape characterization and how can we use this knowledge both when crafting our own original texts or analyzing the writing of others?

Differentiate

To Support:

While providing choice is a wonderful way to engage students, in some cases, too much choice can feel overwhelming or even terrifying. If you have novice or struggling learners, including learners who struggle with anxiety, consider reducing or even eliminating the element of genre choice by instead assigning the new genre to them, complete with sample mentor texts.

Consider ways to provide scaffolds as needed such as:

- Providing visual representations alongside more challenging vocabulary for ESL learners

- Using abridged versions of texts for struggling readers or ESL learners

- Using children's books for the source text (I've found this to be a surprisingly effective strategy for all learners), and

- Allowing students to select whether to work independently or with others.

To Challenge:

Several of the suggestions included in the lesson plan above provide more challenge than others. Embedding additional learning in the form of interview skills, for example, increases the challenge and the rigor of this activity, as does the gaming element that forces students to work with a genre they may not be entirely comfortable with. Student choice is also surprisingly challenging—students must seriously consider the pros and cons of a variety of genres (requiring them to both tap into existing knowledge and analyze the effect of form on content) before they begin writing.

To extend the challenge even further, students could be asked to relocate their character into two or more new genres and then complete a comparative analysis of the changes that occurred in each reimagining of that character.

Suggested Unit Integration:

This activity pairs well with any genre-study unit, be it a single genre such as poetry or drama, or an exploration of a wide range of genres. For lower-level ELA students (grades 9 & 10), a single-study genre exploration may be more effective. For upper-level students (grades 11 & 12 and/or advanced studies students), incorporating more genres into the lesson will increase the challenge and rigor. Here are examples for both scenarios:

- *Grades 9 & 10:* Rather than hosting a single-genre unit on poetry or short stories (both of which are often taught as stand-alone units in lower grade levels for many good reasons), incorporate these genres into a "short narrative writing" unit. In this way, you can incorporate several short, relatively accessible genres into the same unit. Examples of short narrative fiction include: vignettes, poems, extremely short stories, six-word memoirs, short stories of no more than five pages in length, blog posts, online profiles, and playlists.

  Spend some time exploring any combination of these narrative styles before introducing this activity. In anticipation of this lesson, use time at the beginning of your instructional classes to prepare for *The Genre Challenge* lesson. As an example, if you decide to incorporate interview skills into *The Genre Challenge* lesson, you may spend several instructional days embedding interview tasks into your warm-up activities which students can then turn to during *The Genre Challenge* lesson.

  Assessment options for younger students might include:

  o A literary analysis piece for a unit text that explores how the author's use of genre shapes meaning

  o A reflective analysis piece that synthesizes their learning between the unit texts and their own original creations in order to broaden their understanding of the connection between genre and meaning

  o A multimedia presentation that explores the role of genre on meaning

  o A genre competition within or across classes to showcase excellence in genre

- *Grades 11 & 12:* Integrate this activity either at the beginning of the year as a genre review (and pre-assessment opportunity) or at the end of the year as a culminating synthesis learning activity.

If used at the beginning of the school year, spend a few days asking students to review and reflect upon various different genres. This is a good opportunity to assess their prior knowledge and to introduce and discuss less conventional genres such as blogs, podcasts, and the like. Then, conduct this activity to assess the depth of their understanding and/or to push their understanding of genre even deeper.

If used at the end of the school year, spend a few days reviewing the various genres studied over the year and ask the students to sort the texts they've read by genre. Based upon this list, ask students or Writing Teams to source strong passages for each genre from one or more of the readings (they should look for passages or texts that are rich in characterization) and bring them to class on *The Genre Challenge* day. Other students or student groups will work with the student-sourced texts when conducting this activity.

Assessment options for older students might include:

o A short research project into the history of a certain genre or an author who best exemplifies that genre

o A personal narrative that is written in one or more genres (this may be an excellent opportunity to have students write a professional resume and create a carefully curated online profile in preparation for their transition out of high school)

o A "best of" party where students showcase the best examples of both literary and student-created texts based upon a standardized rubric, providing textual evidence to support the award

Extension Activity:

• *Vocabulary:* Rather than providing students with a list of key terms and their definitions at the beginning of the year, have students take ownership of their own Technical Vocabulary

growth by asking students to keep a Technical Vocabulary list that tracks the literary elements/figurative devices you study this year. For each word they identify (in this case, for example, they would include the word "characterization"), they should provide the official definition, a reference to the page in their Writer's Notebook where they can find and review corresponding classroom activities connected with this term, a list of their favorite examples of this device from literature, and an explanation of what features from the examples they find the most compelling. For example, if a student identifies Iago from Shakespeare's, *Othello* as a compelling character, they may explore his complex portrayal, his manipulative nature, etc. (See **Figure 2.12** for a sample Technical Vocabulary assignment sheet).

Figure 2.12

Extension Activity: Technical Vocabulary

Directions: Throughout the school year, you will encounter many technical terms related to literary studies. Some will be familiar and some will be new. It is your job to track and expand upon your understanding of each of these terms.

To accomplish this task, you will maintain a Technical Vocabulary list in your notebook. For each word, include the following:

- ❏ Name of the term/literary device studied
- ❏ Dictionary definition
- ❏ Examples from class readings showcasing your favorite examples of that term in use. Try to capture as many unique and unexpected examples of authors employing this term as you can. For each example you provide, include:
  - ➤ Title/author of the works from where your examples were sourced, along with page numbers, if available
  - ➤ What elements featured in that example you find the most compelling/interesting and why
- ❏ References to the page(s) in your Writer's Notebook where you can find activities connected to our study of this term/literary device
- ❏ Any new or evolving understanding(s) you have of this term as a result of our studies

---

- *Writer's Portfolio:* Extend the learning by having students select one piece from their Writer's Notebook to revise in a new genre as a Publication Piece. As part of the revision, students should reflect upon the original draft and the changes they made based upon their genre selection, as well as a justification as to why their selected genre was the best/most appropriate selection for their reimagined text.

QUARTER 1 CELEBRATION DAY

Congratulations on reaching the end of the first quarter!

Figure 2.13 provides a sample set of instructions for the Quarter 1 Celebration Day event. These instructions envision that a teacher has been embedding the Writing Wednesday lessons into larger instructional units, and therefore, showcase the way that teachers can use the Celebration Day event not only to honor student Writers, but also to extend their learning across a range of skills. You will notice, for example, these instructions move students through the writing process (choosing which piece to revise, what genre to employ, how to organize the Team pieces into one cohesive whole), but the activity also asks students to engage in literary elements such as setting, tone, mood, and ambiguity. In this way, students are asked to synthesize their learning across a range of skills and concepts taught this quarter. If using these instructions to guide your own Celebration Day event, be sure to review the instructions carefully and adjust any of the requirements as desired to align more fully with your own instructional goals.

Figure 2.13

"Seemingly Scary" Celebration Day Expo

Congratulations, Writers. Over the last several weeks, you have been hard at work creating original narratives. Now, you will work with your Writing Team and individually to create your Celebration Day Expo pieces.

Showcase Focus = Fear: What are its causes and how do different people respond to fear?

Team Showcase

Writing Teams will compete to develop and present their Team Showcase which should highlight the best Publication Pieces from your individual members. But there's a twist. Working together, each Team and Team member will revise and organize the individual Publication Pieces to present a carefully curated, unified Team Showcase that, when considered as a whole, tells its own story!

Minimum Requirements: Your Team Showcase must emphasize your learning about stories that are "seemingly scary." To be successful, the Team Showcase piece(s) must:

- Feature a strong sense of setting
- Incorporate a clear and appropriate tone and mood
- Weave in elements of ambiguity in order to create a sense of suspense and/or fear

Form Options: Writing Teams have tremendous flexibility when designing their Team Showcase but there are some key requirements. The Showcase piece must include:

- At least one visual element
- Oral readings of part or all of the narrative
- Meaningful participation during the Expo of each Team member in the final presentation task

Students always have the option to pre-record portions/all of their presentation to ensure full group participation. However, make sure that any pre-recorded components both function correctly (trouble-shoot any technology issues in advance) and that the pre-recorded format serves to advance the narrative objectives of the Writing Team.

Individual Before & After

Contribute to the Team Showcase by proposing several of your draft pieces as candidates for the project. As a team, you will select which of the proposed pieces (at least one from each member) to include in the Writing Expo. Keep track of your revisions and your rationale while you work— you will create an individual "Before-and-After Self-Reflection" project which will be on display gallery style during the Celebration Day.

Figure 2.13 continued

Students will display their individual Before & After pieces gallery style around the room and classmates will explore each student's work after the Team presentations have been completed.

Requirements:
Your Before & After display should include at least two of the earlier drafts of your Publication Piece, complete with annotations showing your changes.

You should also include a written reflection that responds to the following questions:

- Why did you select this piece in connection with the overall group vision?

- What changes did you need to make to better align this text with the Team Showcase goals?

- How did you select the genre for your Publication Piece and how does the genre align with and support both your own writing goals and the goals of your Writing Team?

- What mentor author(s) influenced your approach to this Piece?

- What elements of your Publication Piece are you most proud of? Where did you find success?

- What elements of your Publication Piece show unrealized potential in your Writer's Identity? In other words, what areas of your writing would you like to either target for improvement or experiment with more? Why? What resources, including mentor authors, might you explore to help you achieve your writing goals?

Look Inside Chapter 3

SCAN ME

Scan to access
supplemental
resources

Keeping Time
Prep Time: Low

Description:

We've all heard about time capsules. Some of us have even been lucky enough to take part in either creating a time capsule or opening one that was left behind generations earlier. This activity puts a new spin on a time-honored tradition. For this activity, students first create a time capsule based upon instructions provided by the teacher. If students didn't begin gathering items for this activity in advance (not required) they can simply reflect the spirit of a time capsule by writing their "objects" on strips of paper rather than bringing in tangible items. Then, they pass the time capsule to a neighbor to open. When students open the time capsule, they begin a creative writing narrative based upon a teacher-assigned focus.

For example, if you are conducting a lesson on characterization, you could have the students consider the items in the time capsule in order to develop a character sketch based upon those items. If you are exploring figurative devices, you could ask the student to design a story that employs metaphors or similes by selecting items from the capsule to use as a comparative element in their own original narrative. If the time capsule contains a sweater, for example, and the assignment is to write a story that employs an extended metaphor, the student may write a narrative in which the protagonist's life slowly unravels like a sweater with a loose thread or, alternatively, write a story where seemingly disconnected elements from the protagonist's life are slowly woven together like a sweater.

Student-Friendly Objectives:	*Materials:*
By the end of this lesson, students will be able to: • Consider and select seemingly disconnected elements from an inspiration prompt to develop a unified idea or concept • Write an original narrative that successfully employs the teacher-assigned literary element	• Containers for the student-generated time capsules (enough for however many time capsules you will be assigning). Any container that seals will work so don't be afraid of using something as simple as paper bags, envelopes, or zipper bags • Time capsule filler objects. You may wish to ask students to bring in a collection of items based upon a pre-assigned prompt or have sufficient note paper for students to write their "objects" on slips of paper to add to the time capsule

Rationale:

The beauty of this activity rests on two features: 1) the almost endless ways to customize this lesson and 2) the minimal prep time needed to assign it. You could literally repeat this activity each quarter with different tasks and generate a brand-new experience for the same group of students. What I love most about this activity is that it can be used to target a wide range of skills and concepts while at the same time meeting the needs of diverse learning styles, from abstract to concrete learners, kinesthetic to stationary.

The flexibility of this lesson makes it perfect for deliberate, thoughtful instruction, last-minute planning (not that that ever happens . . .), and even plans for substitutes.

Mix and match this activity to allow for individual, partner, or small group work, or generate your own time capsule in advance and ask all students to pull inspiration from the same capsule.

Anticipatory Activity (15 minutes):

Briefly discuss the idea of a time capsule with students to ensure all students understand the concept. Then, provide the instructions for how students should fill their capsules based on your instructional goals. See **Figure 3.1** for sample instructions on how to fill the time capsule.

Figure 3.1

Filling the Time Capsules

Fill your time capsule with

- Items connected to the setting of your novel.
- Items connected to your life during the past year.
- Items connected to your favorite entertainment product.
- Items connected to the enemies of your protagonist.
- Items connected to the time period of your memoir.
- Newspaper headlines from the past week.
- The names of your favorite songs, books, movies, or podcasts.
- Items that were used in your book as part of the story's conflict.
- Items connected to your childhood that you have since outgrown either physically or emotionally.

You can pre-assign this portion of the activity in the days leading up to this class if you would like to provide more writing time for students.

Provide students with the remaining time to fill their time capsules.

Brainstorm (5 minutes):
Once the time capsules have been filled, ask students to swap time capsules with another student or Writing Team, depending upon your instructional preferences. If you elect to create the time capsule on your own, use this time to have students open the capsule and explore the materials inside.

Provide students with a writing goal for this activity. For example, you may ask students to explore the items in the time capsule and develop a narrative with a strong sense of setting based upon the objects contained in the time capsule, or you may ask students to craft a narrative where two characters are in conflict with one another based upon one or more of the items in the time capsule. **Figure 3.2** provides a list of sample writing prompts to use in connection with this activity.

Figure 3.2

Time Capsule Narrative Instructions

- Explore all of the items uncovered in your time capsule. Then, develop a character sketch for an antagonist using at least x number of items from the capsule as inspiration for your story. Once you have completed your draft, highlight the areas of your story that reflect the time capsule elements.

- Explore all of the items uncovered in your time capsule. Then, develop a narrative in which x number of items trigger a conflict between your characters. The story should be conflict-forward. Once you have completed your draft, highlight the areas of your story that reflect the time capsule elements.

- Explore all of the items uncovered in your time capsule. Then, select one item from the time capsule to use as the comparative element in a short story or a poem that features an extended metaphor. Provide an explanation of how and why you selected your time capsule element for the extended metaphor.

- Explore all of the items uncovered in your time capsule. Then, select one that will serve as a motif that will recur symbolically throughout your narrative.

- Explore all of the items uncovered in your time capsule. Then, develop a narrative that features a protagonist inspired by x number of the items in the capsule and an alternating timeline in which at least one of the time capsule items serves as the link across time. Once you have completed your draft, highlight the character-based elements in one color and the time-travelling elements in another.

Give students about five minutes to review the contents of their time capsule and brainstorm their narrative.

Drafting (50 minutes):
Students will spend fifty minutes drafting their narratives based on your guidance. Use this time to circulate among students and discuss their stories, providing support as needed. If you find that Writers are starting to lose steam, consider adding a new set of required instructions part of the way through to increase the challenge.

Writing Team Share & Reflection (20 minutes):
Students will use the remaining time in class to share their narratives either in whole or in part and then discuss with one another how the instructions affected the direction of their stories.

- What does this activity reveal about the author's selection of details and how do those details affect our understanding of the text?

- What might this activity reveal about everyday inspiration and/or the development of a story?

Differentiate

To Support:	*To Challenge:*
Younger/struggling students may benefit from designing this activity as a partnered or Writing Team task. Rather than having individual students write to the prompt, Teams of students would work together to brainstorm the direction of the story and use their drafting time to either develop a detailed outline of the tale they wish to tell or work collaboratively to develop the full narrative by assigning each member of the Team specific roles intended to support their common narrative goal.	Increase the rigor of this activity by requiring students to weave in multiple literary elements based upon the time capsule. For example, rather than focus exclusively on characterization or figurative devices, you could require students to develop a complex character in a very unique setting who has both an internal and an external conflict based upon one or more item in the time capsule. The more elements you layer into the writing instructions, the more challenging the task becomes. Make the task even more challenging by electing to create a teacher-generated time capsule with at least one "challenge" item that must be included and which serves to make their task even more difficult.

Suggested Unit Integration:

- *Fiction:* Embed this lesson into a fiction unit and ask students to fill their time capsule with features connected to the story. These can be narrow in focus (fill the capsule with elements that connect to the setting, for example) or broad (fill your capsule with items that reflect the complete narrative). You could even increase the challenge here by asking students to fill their capsules with elements that connect to minor features from the story (minor characters, seemingly less important settings, etc.) to consider how authors develop a complete narrative. Then, assign a writing task that either reflects the story you are studying or challenges students to take elements from that story and explore their connection to the broader world by incorporating them into a completely original narrative.

- *Nonfiction:* Ask students to fill their time capsule with elements connected to the historical time period being studied. Then, ask students to write a creative narrative that imagines someone in the future finding the time capsule. What story would they tell (or uncover) based on the objects in the capsule? Increase the challenge by asking students to write a narrative where the future and past intersect based on the items in the capsule.

- *Drama:* Ask students to sketch out a one act play in which x number of the items from the time capsule appear either as plot devices or as props in order to address conventions of drama (see **Figure 3.3** for sample instructions for this unit integration activity).

Figure 3.3

Unit Integration Activity: Dramatic Makeover

Directions: In groups of three to five students, consider the most important elements from your novel to include in your group's time capsule. Remember, these should be concrete, rather than abstract, items such as a key or a photo of a family pet. Once your group has assembled your time capsule, pass your time capsule along to a neighboring group.

Next, open the time capsule which you have just received, exploring its contents and evaluating the significance of each one in connection to the original narrative.

Then, work together as a group to develop a one act play in which you present an updated version of the story, integrating at least three of the time capsule items into your script. You have creative license on how and where to integrate these items: they can function figuratively to symbolize something of larger meaning, or as props for the characters to use, etc. However, they must serve meaningfully to advance the larger narrative. Be sure to incorporate appropriate dramatic elements: dialogue, stage directions, etc., as part of your script.

Your group will perform your one act play for the class. After the performance, each group will submit both a written copy of the script as well as a written rationale that explains the choices you made, including an explanation of how and why you incorporated your chosen time capsule elements into your text.

# Artfulness

Extension Activity:

- *Literary Analysis:* Ask students to consider the items in their time capsule and then connect x number of items to one of the texts previously studied. Then, ask them to write a literary analysis essay in which they consider, for example: In what way does the contents of the time capsule reflect more than one story? What might that reveal about human nature? or: How does each author employ similar devices to achieve a different effect?

- *Research/Nonfiction:* Ask students to research a real-life archeological find and develop an informative research presentation based on their findings. Some questions they may consider: What led to the archeological discovery? How did scientists use their findings to either learn about a culture that had been lost to history or expand upon their understanding of a culture? How are artifacts used in the real world to tell a story? What are the ethical challenges presented by the world of archeology? What are the strengths and limitations of historical artifacts when it comes to understanding a culture?

- *Persuasion:* Ask students to develop a persuasive product based upon one or more of the objects from the time capsule. This can be a simple formative assessment that asks them to develop a persuasive poster using the rhetorical tools they have previously studied or it can be as complex as providing students with a rhetorical situation and a rhetorical goal and then developing an effective advertising campaign based upon their understanding of the rhetorical context.

Color Your World
Prep Time: Medium

Description:
In this activity, students explore a series of artwork that employs strong use of color to consider the connection between color and mood. They then have an opportunity to create their own color art (optional) before using that art or color palettes posted around the room to write a narrative piece that employs skillful diction and other literary elements to capture and convey the mood of their selected color(s).

Student-Friendly Objectives:	*Materials:*
By the end of this lesson, students will be able to:	• Images of selected artwork
• Recognize the connection between tone and mood	• Craft paper and paint or other color tools (optional)
• Convey mood in writing through the careful selection of literary tools	• Various color palette booklets or paint chip sheets

Rationale:
This activity highlights to students the clear connection between visual and written art through a common concept—color. *Color Your World* challenges students to develop their abstract thinking skills by requiring them to consider how best to convey a sense of color without literally employing that color in their narrative. What mood is created by a particular color or color combination? How can mood evolve through the pairing and progression of the (metaphoric) incorporation of various colors into a narrative?

This lesson challenges students to emphasize diction with a focus on tone and mood in order to convey meaning inspired by color connotations. They can also extend their skills acquisition by adjusting their rhythm, punctuation, or use of conflict to convey their selected color(s) as well.

Artfulness

Selecting artwork for the anticipatory activity that showcases one dominant color allows students to see how the same color can be used to convey a variety of moods across the same medium. Any collection of art featuring the same color palette will work here so don't be afraid to experiment with artists and genres.

Anticipatory Activity (20 minutes):

Before students arrive to class, post a variety of artwork showcasing one dominant color scheme such as various pieces from Picasso's Blue Period around the room. These can also be posted as a collage on your classroom's projector if you do not have access to color copies of the art you select.

Ask students to wander around the room exploring each piece both on its own and as part of the larger collection, making notes in the Observation section of their Writer's Notebook.

Initiate a brief whole-class discussion asking them about their observations with a particular focus on how color conveys mood. Be sure to challenge students to point to specific elements of the art they are discussing to support their observations.

Next, provide students with examples of additional artwork from a variety of artists, ensuring that the art selected incorporates color to convey meaning. The more variety of artists, styles, genres, and time periods you can provide, the more options students will have when they move to the writing portion of this lesson. Once students have had a chance to review the additional artwork, initiate a brief class discussion with an emphasis on extending their understanding of how color conveys meaning. For example, ask students to compare and contrast paintings with a different monochrome color scheme or ones that employ multiple colors to get a clearer understanding of how color shapes tone and mood.

Optional Art Activity (10 minutes):

You may elect to have students spend ten minutes creating their own color piece to use as an inspiration for their upcoming writing task. If you elect to incorporate this activity, be sure to stress to students that the goal is to create color inspiration rather than color art, so their focus should be on exploring one color in depth or combining colors into a progression that evolves as the viewer explores the piece, rather than on creating something of particular artistic value.

Optional Visual Inspiration (5 minutes):
Either in combination with the above activity or as a stand-alone option, provide students with tangible color inspiration they can work with on their upcoming writing activity. This can be in the form of color palette booklets like the kind commonly found in the paint section of hardware stores or by providing a selection of paint chips for students to mix and match at will. Once they have selected their chosen colors, they should return to their desks.

Drafting (40 minutes):
Once students have either created or selected their color inspiration, they should brainstorm the mood(s) conveyed by their color choices as well as a list of key words that might help convey that mood. Then, they should begin outlining a story that matches their color selection. For example, if they selected to work with various shades of red, they may write an upbeat, energetic, or possibly even angry narrative. If they selected a variety of colors—perhaps yellow, blue, and orange—they might write a narrative that conveys an evolving mood that matches that progression of colors. Once they have completed their pre-writing activities, they should use the remainder of this time for drafting.

Writing Team Share (10 minutes):
After their drafting time ends, have students share the stories with their Writing Team without telling their Writing Team what color(s) they used for inspiration. After each reading, the Writing Team should attempt to guess which color(s) the piece was inspired by based on the diction, tone, and mood of the piece.

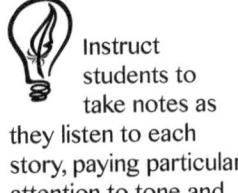 Instruct students to take notes as they listen to each story, paying particular attention to tone and mood signals. They can use those notes to fuel the post-reading discussion.

Reflection (5 minutes):
Students should spend the final five minutes of class reflecting on how this process shaped their understanding of tone and mood and how they can use this knowledge when crafting future writing pieces.

- How did their word choice change as a result of the color(s) they selected?

- How were they able to capture a mood connected to either one shade of color or spanning a variety of colors?

- What other techniques did they employ in their narrative to align with their color choices (e.g., syntax, conflict, characterization, etc.)?

Differentiate

Not everyone sees color the same way. Spend some time as a class connecting colors (by name rather than by image) to tones and moods. This provides a control element to keep the task unified and accessible for all students.

To Support:
Spread this lesson over two days to support younger/struggling learners. Once you have explored the art in detail (add more time for class discussion to this step as an additional scaffold), transition to an exploration of writing samples that convey a strong sense of mood. Ask students to work in their Writing Team to determine what color(s) best match each sample text and why. Be sure to annotate for literary elements, with a special emphasis on diction, that supports their findings. Then, dedicate the entire second day to the writing task, building in more time for Writing Team shares and discussions (and perhaps including a mid-way break for Writing Team conferences during the drafting stage) to allow students additional time to process their learning.

To Challenge:
Turn this into a "forced" writing activity where students are given the color to write to at the beginning of the task and then are required to layer in either different shades of the same color or various new colors, adjusting the tone/mood of their narrative to reflect the new color choices.

Alternatively, follow the original directions above but ask students to create their own custom artwork after they have finished drafting that visually demonstrates, in sequence, the progression of their color choices. Once their art dries, they will need to add quotes and excerpts from their own writing in the various color fields to support their visual interpretation of their own writing.

Suggested Unit Integration:
This is a great activity to incorporate into any unit where tone and mood are being explored. Select passages from your whole-class reading to annotate for diction, syntax, and other style choices as may be desired, and ask students to consider what color the author seems to be writing in. Require students to support their argument with textual evidence and use the class discussions to reinforce how authors use diction, syntax, and other literary elements to shape

meaning and convey emotion. This activity can also work with texts that convey a strong sense of setting—for example, creepy houses, dilapidated buildings, cheerful gardens, etc. Extend the learning further by comparing and contrasting passages from your readings that seem to convey different tones and moods and then exploring how the contrast of those two "colors" shapes the reader's understanding of the larger narrative.

Extension Activity:

- *Poetry Analysis:* Ask students to "color map" a complex poem, identifying what color(s) best fit the various portions of the poem and how the author uses diction, syntax, or other literary elements to convey the tone and mood. Once they have mapped their text, ask them to write a literary analysis essay that explores how the author's use of tone and mood shapes meaning (see **Figure 3.4** for sample instructions for this extension activity).

Figure 3.4

Extension Activity: Poetry Analysis

Directions: Carefully read and annotate the provided poem. Then, based upon your observations about the poet's use of tone and mood, color map your poem to accurately convey the shifts present in the text. Make sure you can justify why you selected each color—including various shades of the same color—with textual evidence from the poem.

Once you have annotated and color-mapped your poem, consider the effect of the poet's choices:

- How does the poet use literary elements such as diction, syntax, and imagery to convey a tone or a mood?
- How does the poet use shifts in tone and mood to structure the evolution of ideas presented in this poem?
- What does the evolution of the tone and mood of the poem suggest about the poem's message?
- Overall, what message is being presented in this poem?

Finally, use your findings to craft a literary analysis essay in which you argue how your poet uses literary elements to convey meaning with a special focus on diction, tone, and mood.

Artfulness

- *Multimedia:* Ask students to develop a mood board that captures their selected color(s) using excerpts from their own original narrative as well as sample excerpts from various other texts that, through their use of diction, syntax, and/or other literary elements, reflect a similar color palette.

- *Research:* Ask students to select a color and then research the symbolism of that color across various cultures and regions of the world. Alternatively, ask students to research how various artists have employed that color to support their creations with an emphasis on how they employ color to shape meaning.

Artfulness
Prep Time: Medium

Description:

This lesson puts the "art" in Language Arts by asking students to revisit a previous draft and take it through a revision round with the goal of matching their own original narrative to a piece of inspiration art. With this activity, students will conduct a gallery walk to explore various different pieces of artwork and then review their Writer's Notebook to find a draft that could be modified to capture the essence or the spirit of their inspiration art.

Student-Friendly Objectives:	*Materials:*
By the end of this lesson, students will be able to: • Evaluate their own writing to identify areas for revision • Use inspiration from their environment to develop and strengthen their own writing	• Various color copies of artwork

Rationale:

Too often our students are afraid to take risks. Afraid of being "wrong" or eager to earn the A, students opt for the safe path and produce writing that feels formulaic and familiar. This activity challenges those tendencies by forcing students to play with their writing in unique and unconventional ways. Rather than using the revision task here as a way of improving the mechanics of their writing (which is, of course, a worthy goal), this lesson instead uses the revision task as a way of playing with their writing—experimenting, mixing and matching— in short, taking risks. Because this revision is still, at heart, a draft that lives in the Writer's Notebook, there is no fear of being wrong and no risk to their class grade. Therefore, students are more willing to focus on the artistic elements of their writing rather than the technical elements.

 *Artfulness*

What makes this Writing Wednesday lesson so special is that students select the art they want to work with for their inspiration. Students select the draft they think best fits. Students make the creative revisions necessary to align the two in a meaningful manner. Students are in control of their learning.

Without realizing it, by completing this activity, students are engaging in the critical thinking skills necessary to drive unique, original, deliberate writing, thus developing their authentic Writer's Voice while avoiding the pitfalls inherent in graded revision work.

Anticipatory Activity (30 minutes):
Before students arrive, either post artwork around the room gallery style or create Rotation Stations with various different artwork and artistic mediums accessible to students. (The Rotation Station format may work best if you are providing non-visual art such as music or dramatic skits as part of the inspiration gallery).

Don't be afraid to have your students do some of the heavy lifting. Rather than selecting the artwork for this activity yourself, in the weeks leading up to the activity, ask your students to bring in images of their favorite pieces of art. Set a deadline in advance of this Writing Wednesday lesson so you can review their submissions and determine how best to display them. Then, use the student-curated collection to serve as inspiration for the whole class.

Figure 3.5

Sample Inspirational Art Genres

Canvas Painting	Sculpture	Museum Artifact
Music	Spoken Poetry	Photography
Woven Quilts/Tapestries	Murals	Street/Graffiti Art
Magazine Advertisements	Cartoons	Architecture
Book/Album Covers	Set Design (for stage plays)	Graphic/Digital Art

---

Ask students to explore each inspiration piece, taking notes in the Observation section of their Writer's Notebook.

Once students have had a chance to explore all of the inspiration art, they should select the top three exemplars that they would like to work with for today's activity. Then, they review their Writer's Notebook to find drafts that they think they may be able to successfully revise to reflect some element of the inspiration art they selected. They will ultimately only be working with one draft and one piece of art, but initially, they select three to give them options when they review their

Writer's Notebook. If students discover that none of their existing drafts would work with their selected art, they are welcome to reevaluate the inspiration art to find a better fit.

Brainstorm (10 minutes):
Once students have selected their inspiration art and an appropriate draft, they will begin brainstorming how best to revise their draft to fit the new context. They are welcome to explore any element of their chosen art that inspires them—the format, the genre, the colors, the shape, even the mood or abstract ideas conveyed by that art. They should begin outlining or annotating their original draft in accordance with their brainstorming ideas.

Revision (40 minutes):
Students will spend forty minutes revising their original draft to reflect their inspiration art. If they paired a draft, for example, with a piece of music, they may spend their revision time adjusting their diction, rhythm, and syntax to better reflect the musical quality of their inspiration song. If they selected a piece of visual art, they may revise their writing to reflect the story depicted in the painting, or one of the subjects of the art. The options for students are limitless, but they will need to be able to explain how their revisions capture some element of their inspiration art.

Reflection (10 minutes):
Students spend the final ten minutes reflecting in their Writer's Notebook on how this process affected their draft.

- What art served as their inspiration?

- How did they select the draft they would revise for this task based on that artwork?

- What revision elements did they need to focus on in order to align with their inspiration piece?

- How does their revision reflect the inspiration piece?

Artfulness

Students should reference specific elements from both the inspiration art and their own draft to support their response to the final question.

Differentiate

To Support:	*To Challenge:*
Younger/struggling learners are often overwhelmed by too many choices. For these learners, I would recommend limiting your inspiration art both in quantity and in variety of formats. You may also wish to break this activity up into two days, providing conference time for students on the first day both in their Writing Teams and one-on-one if needed to help them work through their options and brainstorm their best strategy. The second day can be spent focusing on the revision process, building in additional conference time to help students who may be struggling.	Ask students to blend inspiration from two or more art pieces into their writing and increase the challenge further by requiring the two inspiration pieces to represent different genres, styles, and/or formats. For example, students may be challenged to revise their own draft to reflect some element of both Van Gogh's *Starry Night* and Lakeside's song, "Fantastic Voyage."

Suggested Unit Integration:

This is a great activity to weave into a lesson on the writing process. As students are working on select essays or other drafts of non-creative writing pieces that will ultimately be submitted for a grade, spend some time exploring drafts, revisions, or alternative versions of texts by published authors or artists. Examples might include the multiple drafts of Pablo Picasso's artistic sketch, *The Bull*, the two different versions of Mary Shelley's novel, *Frankenstein*, or excerpts from the different translations of Elie Wiesel's memoir, *Night*.

Comparing and contrasting alternative examples of mentor texts allows students to see the artistic—and sometimes unexpected—revision choices that creators can take as they develop their work. As you discuss the various versions of the texts that you explore, carefully moderate the discussions to focus students' attention on the creative, artistic changes that the writer selects and how those changes affect the way the reader/

viewer understands the work. In addition to priming students for the *Artfulness* Writing Wednesday activity, this approach also focuses their attention on the creative—rather than the technical—revisions Writers should consider when undertaking the revision process.

Extension Activity:

- *Definition Essay:* Introduce students to Definition Essays and then ask them to develop a Definition Essay that explores a term connected to today's lesson, such as "art," "inspiration," or "revision."

- *Drama:* Ask students to select a famous work of art and then update it by incorporating it in a meaningful manner into a one act play or ask students to select a series of famous art to link together into a story and then develop the story created by those art pairings into a one act play.

- *Multimedia Presentation/Self-Reflection:* Ask students to develop a multimedia presentation that reveals the writing process they went through as they created a Publication Piece. Their presentation should include the prompt, the brainstorming stage, and at least two rounds of revision that showcase both the creative and the technical revisions they made. They should also have a section that discusses the editing stage (this will force students to recognize, on their own, the difference between revision and editing and why both components are important to the writing process). Their presentation should conclude with a reflection that explores how the writing process strengthened their final product and what they are most proud of. If they have any continuing concerns or frustrations with their draft, they are welcome to explore those as part of their reflection as well (see **Figure 3.6** for sample instructions for this extension activity and scan the QR code at the beginning of this chapter to access an editable scoring rubric for that assessment).

Figure 3.6

Extension Activity: Multimedia Presentation

Congratulations on having crafted your Publication Piece. We know you have been working hard to bring your vision to life. Now, it's time for you to reflect upon your writing journey with us, sharing your successes and your struggles to showcase how far you've come.

Requirements: Develop a multimedia presentation in which you reveal:

- The prompt that inspired your creation;
- Examples of your brainstorming process;
- Excerpts from your work that showcase (complete with a rationale) at least two significant before-and-after examples of the creative revisions you undertook during this process;
- Excerpts from your work that showcase (complete with a rationale) at least two before-and-after examples of the editing you undertook during this process (grammar, punctuation, etc.);
- A self-reflection that explores how the writing process strengthened your final product, what you struggled with during the writing process and how you overcame those struggles, what you are most proud of, and what continuing frustrations, if any, you still have with your work that you would like to improve upon if you had more time.

The Format: As with most of our creative tasks, you have tremendous artistic license with the format of your presentation. The only "rules" are that you include both written and visual elements, you incorporate some element of oral reading into your class presentation, your work is school-appropriate, and that you incorporate all of the bulleted requirements outlined above.

Remember, however, that I can only score you based upon the evidence you provide. It is up to you to ensure that you are providing sufficient evidence to earn the score you would like.

- *Research Multimedia Essay:* Ask students to research and report upon a famous work of art that has been alluded to or updated at various times in history. A great example is Edvard Munch's, *The Scream,* which has appeared in countless television shows and movies and now lives as an emoji in various media platforms. Other examples include Abbott and Costello's "Who's on First?" skit which is frequently updated in pop culture, or the modern retelling of Shakespeare's, *The Taming of the Shrew* featured in the 1999 film, *10 Things I Hate About You.*

- *Vocabulary:* Ask students to update their Technical Vocabulary sheet to include the word "art" and then ask them to broaden their definition to incorporate elements introduced and/or discussed in today's activity. Other definitions to consider including or revising: draft, edit, inspiration, revise, writing process.

Making Time
Prep Time: Medium

Description:
In this lesson, students will learn how to expand a moment in writing in order to bring in elaborative details that shape the overall narrative. First, they will compare and contrast two passages from a fictional text —one that has been edited to strip out elaborative details to shrink the narrative and one that represents the author's original work, where the elaborative details are fully fleshed out. Students will consider the effect of both versions before progressing to a practice activity that asks them to expand a moment from a sample passage by adding details that force the reader to pause at that moment—thus, "making" time.

Student-Friendly Objectives:
By the end of this lesson, students will be able to:

- Recognize how elaboration affects writing and shapes the direction of a larger narrative
- Expand a moment to control the perception of time in their own writing

Materials:

- Two versions of an excerpt of your choice—one that has been stripped to its barest components and one that represents the complete, elaborative version
- Copies of writing passages for students to expand

Rationale:
A key element to close reading is considering the effect of the author's selection of details. Where does the author condense time to speed up the pace or withhold information from the reader? Where does the author slow down and expand a moment? What do these choices, including choices regarding what to include in the expanded moments, reveal about the larger narrative? This can be a difficult skill to teach students through reading alone. Forcing them to create the expansion content—to select for themselves what details to add to a narrative —will demonstrate to them the value of small details. In addition, students will need to determine where to slow down time, thus recognizing the effect of controlling time in their own compositions to achieve their writing goals.

Their understanding is further strengthened by assigning each member of the Writing Team a different literary element to focus on for their elaboration task while using the same original condensed excerpt as the control.

During the share, they will come to appreciate how shifting the approach can affect the narrative, and its meaning, in significant ways.

Anticipatory Activity (15 minutes):
Arrange students into their Writing Teams and provide each Team with two versions of the same narrative—one that has been edited to condense it to its barest form and another that expands upon the moment being depicted in order to layer in narrative details with the effect of slowing the perception of time. In their Writing Teams, students compare and contrast both versions, taking notes in the Observation section of their Writer's Notebook. Use the QR code at the front of this chapter to access sample paired passages to use for this activity.

A brief whole-class discussion should follow that explores their findings with an emphasis on how the different versions affect our understanding of the narrative, including our understanding of time.

Process (10 minutes):
Provide each student or Writing Team the same passage from a different narrative of your choice. The passage should be short enough to contain minimal details, but long enough to provide multiple options for where to expand the narrative.

Then, provide each Writing Team (or each member of individual Writing Teams) with a different expansion focus. For example, one student may be asked to expand the moment to enhance characterization while another might be asked to expand upon the setting or develop a literary conflict. Provide students with a few minutes to brainstorm the best approach to this task—what details might they include based upon their assigned expansion focus and where in the existing passage is the best place to insert these details?

Drafting (40 minutes):
Students spend the next forty minutes expanding the moment to "make time," revising as they work if desired (for example, students may realize as they begin working that a different moment from the passage would be a better fit for their expansion choices). At the end of their drafting time, have students write a bulleted outline of possible directions the rest of the narrative may head based upon the changes they made (i.e., if the story were expanded further, would the reader follow a character, a conflict, an idea, etc., and how does that direction connect back directly to the choices they made when expanding their moment?).

Writing Team/Whole-Class Share (20 minutes):
Depending on how you designed the activity, have students share either within their Writing Teams or across Writing Teams to read their expansion creations. After each student reads their revised passage, students should compare and contrast the various creations to discuss the effect of "making time" within a narrative. **Figure 3.7** provides Writing Teams a focus for their discussions.

Figure 3.7

How did the expansion focus affect the readers' perception of time?

How did the expansion focus affect the selection of details included in this longer moment?

Reflection (5 minutes):
Based on the preceding share, students should reflect in their Writer's Notebook on the effect of expanding a moment through the development of narrative details.

- What have they learned about controlling time in a story?

- How might they use this knowledge in upcoming writing tasks?

Differentiate

To Support:

To support younger/struggling learners, provide a graphic organizer to assist students during the brainstorming stage (before they begin drafting their own narrative expansion). Make sure the graphic organizer asks questions that help them focus on their assigned expansion focus. For example, if students are expanding to develop character, ask questions that get them thinking about what may motivate the character, what that character might be thinking as they survey their scene, how the character might interact with the setting, who or what the character may be in conflict with, etc. Have students collaborate with one or more members of their Writing Team when selecting where in the passage to expand the moment, considering the effect of each of their choices on both the organization and flow of the story as well as the effect it may have on the reader's perception of the larger narrative.

To Challenge:

Mix and Match: Enhance the critical thinking required to complete this task by providing students with a variety of passages and expansion focuses to select from and then have them review each one to determine how best to proceed by matching one passage to one expansion focus and providing a rationale for their choices as part of the reflection process.

Increase the challenge even further by requiring that all members of the Writing Team select from the same mix and match options but require that each option can only be used once. (Note: This means that each individual component —as opposed to each individual pairing—can only be used once).

Suggested Unit Integration:

This activity pairs really well with any close reading exploration you are conducting in your instructional units. Pair this lesson with a text that is dense in elaborative details to encourage critical thinking of how or why those details shape the reader's understanding of the larger narrative. Use one of the whole-class texts you are working with for your instructional units when selecting your passages to explore and expand in order to enhance the connection further. Conduct a before-and-after analysis activity by exploring the same close reading passage during your instructional days both before and after completing this activity to measure students' growth with this skill. **Figure 3.8** explores the multiple assessment opportunities provided by integrating *Making Time* into your larger instructional units.

Figure 3.8

Unit tie-ins for these writing activities often provide rich assessment material. Consider, for example, the assessment options outlined below. If you elected to incorporate all of these suggested activities (which envision Edgar Allen Poe's "The Fall of the House of Usher" as the unit text), this one Writing Wednesday activity can provide no fewer than four assessment opportunities spanning no fewer than three different writing skills: literary analysis, comparative analysis, and narrative writing.

Literary Analysis Pre-Assessment: Students read and analyze the introductory paragraphs from "The Fall of the House of Usher" and then write a one-paragraph literary analysis in which they argue how the author uses narrative details to establish the setting.

Literary Analysis Summative Assessment: After students have completed the unit lessons, including this *Making Time* activity, they will write another one-paragraph literary analysis using the same passage and prompt as the control to capture the evolution of their understanding.

Comparative Analysis Assessment for Self-Reflection: Instruct students on comparative analysis, including the three main formats for organizing comparative pieces: cause and effect, point-by-point, and block. Then, ask students to conduct a comparative analysis self-reflection of their own pre- and post-assessment analysis. They should craft their self-reflection as a comparative analysis argument in which they explore their progress with understanding the skills taught during the unit.

- Bonus Assessment Opportunity: As part of their submission, require students to provide a written rationale explaining why they selected their chosen comparative analysis organizational format to demonstrate their understanding of the different organizational structures and how they affect the reader's understanding of the text.

Narrative Elements Publication Piece Writing Assessment: Conclude the unit by having students write their own original short fiction (ideally by revising an existing Writer's Notebook draft) in which they deliberately expand a moment through the careful selection of details.

- Bonus Assessment Opportunity: As part of their submission, require students to provide a written rational explaining their writing goals for this piece and how the *Making Time* details they integrated into their writing were used to support that purpose.

Extension Activity:

- *Comparative Analysis:* Provide students with excerpts from two different texts (ideally ones that share a similar controlling element such as character or setting). One passage should be rich with elaborative details that slow down the moment. The other should contain sparse details. Students compare and contrast the approach of each author and then write a comparative analysis

essay in which they argue how authors use a selection of details to inform the reader's understanding of the text.

Pulling an excerpt from a text that students have not previously encountered will ensure that they are closely-reading the details the author provides, and not inadvertently relying on memories of previous discussions to fuel their findings.

- *Literary Analysis:* Provide students with a lengthy passage (about one full, typed page) from a text. Select a passage that is rich in narrative details (as opposed to dialogue) and where a moment seems to be expanded upon. Then, provide students with a prompt that requires them to argue how the author's selection of details develops a complex relationship or reveals a literary conflict.

- *Publication Piece:* Have students revisit one of their own original drafts and develop that draft either into a full-length short story or a lengthy vignette (at least one typed page in length) that develops complexity through the expansion of a moment and the careful selection of details. As part of their submission, students should include a reflection that explores how they selected their draft to revise, what their writing goals were with this revision, how they attempted to meet those goals through their selection of detail, and how the narrative changed from the original to the revised draft.

Who Says?
Prep Time: Low

Description:
In this activity, students begin writing their own original narrative based upon a story prompt provided by the teacher. Roughly mid-way through their writing time, however, they are forced to exchange their work with someone who is not on their Writing Team. They then read that student's draft and incorporate the narrative perspective (POV) of one of the characters in that student's story into their own narrative to explore how narrative perspective shapes meaning.

Student-Friendly Objectives:	*Materials:*
By the end of this lesson, students will be able to:	• Story-starting prompt(s)
• Write a multi-perspective narrative	
• Understand how narrative point of view shapes meaning	

Rationale:
This low-prep activity challenges students to consider multiple perspectives when crafting their own original narratives. Although the activity begins easily enough—simply write a narrative based upon a writing prompt—students soon realize that the only way they can accomplish their task is by taking the perspectives of others into account.

Requiring students to read a partner's work accomplishes a variety of academic tasks including: having an opportunity to share their work with others in a low-stress, low-stakes manner; being provided with authentic audiences for their drafts; and broadening their own perspectives by valuing and incorporating the perspectives of others in a meaningful way into their own work.

By the end of this activity, students will have had an opportunity to draft, share, and revise their own original narrative and will have gained experience writing multi-perspective narratives, thus deepening their understanding of how POV shapes meaning.

Artfulness

Anticipatory Activity: (5 minutes):
Play a song that incorporates multiple perspectives such as The Human League's, "Don't You Want Me?" Ask students to listen to the song carefully and, at its conclusion, lead a brief whole class discussion about how the addition of the second perspective shapes the listener's understanding of the story.

Process (5 minutes):
Provide students with a story prompt to get them started with their drafting. You can develop your own story prompt for the entire class to work with or you can provide individual prompts by using story-generating cards. Because this is an exercise in perspective, make sure the prompt requires characters to appear in the narrative.

Drafting (25 minutes):
Allow students to begin drafting their stories based on the prompts you provided. Do not interrupt them, simply let them work. Ensure that all students are writing efficiently during the time provided as they will need to have a reasonable amount written by the time they exchange their story with their neighbor.

Discovery (10 minutes):
After students have been writing for a period of time, interrupt them by instructing the students to exchange their Notebooks with someone in the class who is not a member of their Writing Team.

Student pairs then swap stories, reading each other's stories silently. After they read the story once, they should go back through the story with a focus on characterization—what characters have been developed in their partner's story, and which of these characters may work well in their own story? Students should take notes in the Observation section of their Writer's Notebook to refer to as needed when they begin revising.

Drafting (25 minutes):
Students now return to their narrative but must determine how and where to effectively switch perspectives so that the character they

Every once in a while, you will have a student in the classroom who either refuses to write or who does not write a sufficient amount of text prior to the exchange. If this happens, the other student will not have enough material to work with when it comes time to insert a different perspective into their own stories. I recommend having a handful of excerpts from sample narratives available that you can provide to partners who may have insufficient inspiration material for the second half of the activity. In a pinch, you can ask students to incorporate a perspective pulled from a unit text or even from a perspective gleaned by exploring books from the class bookshelf.

selected from their partner's story is now narrating their own tale. They should consider:

- How will they make the transition between narrative POV so as not to jar the reader or destroy the cohesion of the original narrative?

- How will this new POV affect the overall meaning of the work as a whole?

- What adjustments will they need to make to their original drafting plan to create a unified narrative with this new character and, importantly, this new character's POV?

Partner Share (10 minutes):
Rather than sharing with their Writing Teams, students will spend ten minutes reading their finished draft to their POV partner. In this manner, students see their work celebrated both in their own original narrative as well as in their partner's work, and they get a sense of the options one has when incorporating narrative POV. As part of their share, they should discuss why they selected that particular character, what understanding of that character they gleaned from the original narrative, and how they incorporated that understanding into their own story to form a cohesive narrative.

Reflection (10 minutes):
Students spend the final ten minutes in their Writer's Notebook reflecting on the process.

- How difficult was it to select and incorporate a brand new POV into their own original narrative?

- What challenges did they encounter, for example, with genre or style?

- How did they decide what elements from their inspiration character to weave into their own narrative?

- How did the direction of their overall narrative change as a result of the new POV?

 By this point in the school year, students should be fairly comfortable with their Writing Teams. While this is by design and is an important component of their growth as Writers, it is also important that they periodically be given a chance to explore and celebrate the writing of students who are not part of their Writing Team. Changing up their writing partners for this activity provides students an opportunity to broaden their own perspectives by listening to fresh voices within their classroom.

Differentiate	
To Support: Support younger/struggling students by adapting the partner share stage to include a collaborative brainstorming stage. In this variation, partners build in discussion time to consider the element(s) of each story that might harmonize with one another and use that as a starting place when considering which character each student should incorporate into their writing. Partners can also work collaboratively to brainstorm how and where in each narrative it may make sense to switch POV and any other revision suggestions they can think of to better incorporate the new POV.	**To Challenge:** Increase the challenge by layering in one additional "forced" element. Once students have exchanged their work with one partner, they should exchange their work again with a new partner, read their narrative, and incorporate one of that student's settings or other literary elements into their own writing along with the character from their first partner.

Suggested Unit Integration:

This activity pairs well with any study connected to narrative POV. Include this early in the year to force students to think beyond simply identifying and labeling POV when considering its impact on meaning. Include this activity later in the year when studying more challenging texts that incorporate alternating POVs, such as Mark Zusak's. *The Book Thief* or Julia Alvarez's, *In the Time of the Butterflies*. Once students have completed this activity, have them revisit their whole class reading to consider the effect of each individual perspective included in the narrative, where the POV shifts, and how the authorial choices affect the reader's understanding of the story.

Extension Activity:

- *Literary Analysis:* When paired with a whole class reading, ask students to write a literary analysis essay that explores how the author's use of narrative POV shapes the reader's understanding of the work as a whole.

- *Nonfiction:* Ask students to compare and contrast news stories about a current event by reading articles written by opposing media sources (e.g., those leaning conservative and liberal, those based in the US and those based in other countries, etc.). Students should compare and contrast how each event is portrayed with a special emphasis on analyzing how perspective affects the story's portrayal in each news outlet (for example, whose perspective does the journalist seem to favor when portraying the story and how might that choice reflect the journalistic perspective of the source outlet?). **Figure 3.9** provides sample instructions for this extension activity.

Figure 3.9

Extension Activity: Nonfiction Comparative Analysis

We have seen how narrative perspective controls and shapes a reader's understanding of a text. Now, you will explore how perspective shapes our understanding of the world as well. Select a topic connected to some element inspired by your novel. Then, conduct research to see how that topic has been covered in the news.

Instructions: Identify at least two contrasting news sources (for example, sources that skew liberal or conservative, sources that represent different regions of the world, or sources that represent the evolution of the coverage of that topic over time).

Compare and contrast how the topic is covered in each source, considering, for example:

- What overall story is being told in each article (how might you summarize the story?)
- Whose perspective is emphasized?
- Whose perspective is minimized?
- What element(s) of the story are given importance?
- What element(s) of the story are minimized?
- What details does each source include in the story and how do those details inform the reader's understanding of the topic?
- What images are associated with each story? How do those images function rhetorically to support the story's focus?
- How do the image captions serve to inform the reader's understanding?

Based on your comparison, develop a multimedia presentation in which you present your findings to the class. Your presentation should include:

- Copies of each article (or links for viewers to explore each article on their own)
- Your detailed comparative findings
- An exploration of how readers may come to understand that topic based upon your analysis
- Properly formatted citations for all sources referenced in your presentation

---

- *Persuasion:* Have students create a set of persuasive posters on a pro/con issue. One poster should persuade viewers to the "pro" side of the issue and the other poster should persuade viewers to the "con" side of the issue. Students should incorporate the rhetorical tools studied in class as part of the poster development, but their choices should be informed by the perspective of their fictional speaker.

- *Publication Piece—Poetry:* Ask students to demonstrate their understanding of POV by writing "perspective" poems such as poems for two voices, poems that hint at multiple perspectives modeled after poems such as Stevie Smith's, "Not Waving But Drowning," poems that hint at a lack of perspective such as Edwin Arlington Robinson's poem, "Richard Cory," or poems that seem to speak to one another in meaningful ways such as William Blake's "The Tyger" and "The Lamb."

QUARTER 2 CELEBRATION DAY

Congratulations on reaching the mid-way point in the school year!

By the end of the second marking period, students should be ready for a bit more of a challenge. You will notice that the sample instructions for this quarter ask students to continue working with the tone, mood, and genre exploration they began in quarter one. It also spirals their understanding of multimedia presentations by requiring students to select a delivery format for their Team Showcase that is not slide-dependent. Finally, the Quarter 2 Celebration Day instructions advance student learning by challenging them to incorporate multiple narrative perspectives and style elements such as diction and syntax to start highlighting a broader range of literary elements that factor into writing.

Figure 3.10

QUARTER 2 CELEBRATION DAY

Congratulations, Writers! In this marking period, you have learned about important literary elements such as selection of detail, elaboration, tone, mood, genre, and narrative perspective. Now, it's time to celebrate your learning.

Work with your Writing Team to consider a shared topic of interest and develop a multimedia exploration connected to that topic.

The Group Task:

As a Team, select one topic of common interest to explore in-depth. Then, consider this topic thoroughly, being careful to consider the topic in a variety of ways:

- What are the various positions associated with this topic (e.g., what are people for or against in connection to this topic)?
- What are the relative strengths and weaknesses of each of these positions?
- What is the range of perspectives—particularly opposing or contrasting perspectives—connected to this topic?
- What are the feelings (tones/moods) likely associated with each of these perspectives?
- Where have you seen this topic explored in the real world? (For example, books, movies, music, news articles, advertisements, etc.)

Based on your responses to the questions above, as well as any other questions you feel may be useful in developing this project, assign each Team member one unique perspective and genre in which to write, with the goal of developing a multimedia presentation that spans a range of viewpoints connected to your topic. The individual pieces should be designed to harmonize with one another to develop a cohesive exploration of your topic, but you should carefully consider the strengths and interests of each Writer when determining what components to build into your presentation.

On the Celebration Day, your Team members will present your full exploration to the class—but there's a catch: <u>You cannot use a slide-show format to deliver your presentation</u>. Therefore, think carefully about alternative presentation formats and select the one best suited to your objectives.

The Individual Task:

Once your unique perspective and genre have been determined, review your Writer's Notebook to find drafts that could be revised to fit this new vision or develop a new draft with your individual and group goal in mind. Then, take that piece through appropriate revisions to develop your writing into the Publication Piece which will be included as part of your Team's presentation.

Figure 3.10 continued

Suggested genres:

Documentary Poems	Poems for Two Voices	Multi-Perspective Poetry	Vignettes or Short Fiction
Epistolary-Style Narratives	Photo Essays	Magazine Advertisements	Graphic Narratives
Song Lyrics	Podcasts	Short Films	One-Act Plays

Submission Requirements:

Group Submission: Each Team will submit one (1) copy of their presentation for a group assessment score.

Individual Submission: Each Team member will submit their individual self-reflection for an assessment score. As part of your reflection, be sure to address:

- How the brainstorming stage of the activity informed the selection of your own unique perspective and genre, including how your individual piece connected to and supported the shared vision of the larger Writing Team

- What message you were hoping to convey with your individual piece (your writing objective), and

- How you employed narrative perspective, genre, tone, and mood to meet your writing objective.

Look Inside Chapter 4

Scan to access
supplemental
resources

Inspired by a True Story
Prep Time: Medium

Description:

In this lesson, students learn how writers often find inspiration in the real world. Students begin with an anticipatory activity that gets them focused on the various ways different viewers interpret the same event. Then, students explore photos from real-life newspapers to find inspiration for their own fictional narratives.

Student-Friendly Objectives:
By the end of this lesson, students will be able to:

- Recognize that writing inspiration comes from a wide-variety of sources
- Understand the difference between stories that are "based upon a true story" and those "inspired by a true story"

Materials:

- A handful of charade-style prompts that are inspired by real-world events in the news, folded up and placed inside a hat to be selected at random
- One or more outgoing students (there are usually a few in each class) who will conduct the opening activity
- Class copies of one or more photos pulled from recent newspaper articles with only their captions provided

Rationale:

As educators, we know that words matter and, in particular, small words matter. Students, however, are often so accustomed to reading quickly that small details such as the difference between "based upon" and "inspired by" often get overlooked. This can lead to confusion about the role of the stories they hear in their own lives.

This activity forces students to recognize and understand the difference between phrasing and how these small but important diction choices shape our understanding of a narrative. By creating their own stories "inspired by true events" students have a chance to experience first-hand the wide variety of stories that the real word can inspire and, as a consequence, they will become more sensitive to the way language operates to shape meaning.

Anticipatory Activity (20 minutes):

As students enter the classroom, pull one or more students aside and ask them to help with an opening charades-style activity (you can pre-arrange this with students in the class period preceding today's lesson to save time). When selecting students, try to choose those who are naturally outgoing and/or creative and who would have fun with this type of activity. Be careful to select students you feel confident will be respectful in their interpretations—the last thing you want is for a seemingly harmless prompt to go wrong because of the way the students choose to act it out.

The students who you selected at the beginning of class will now pull a scenario from a hat. Once they have their scenario(s), send those students into the hallway for two minutes to brainstorm how they will deliver their skit.

While they are brainstorming, ask the remaining students to pull out their Writer's Notebook. Instruct them to watch the upcoming skit carefully, making note of anything and everything that captures their attention during the skit, whether the attention-grabbing details come directly from the charades game or from other features/elements around the room.

Students then watch the brief performance of the skit (two to five minutes). Afterward, ask students to imagine they are creating a social media post and to write the story of that event. Provide students with five minutes to draft their social media "post."

Then, ask for volunteers or call on a few select students to share their social media posts verbatim. Before they begin reading, they should state: "The following is inspired by a true story."

Anticipated Outcome: Although students will have watched the same skit, it is likely that different students will have written about entirely different events. This is more likely if you suggest to students ahead of time that anything in the classroom that they observe is fair game to write about—chances are some students will be looking beyond the action of the skit and will capture different details.

Artfulness

Whole Class Share: After you have heard a variety of responses, ask students to try to guess what the real inspiration event was or provide that information to them. Then, ask them to consider what the range of "inspired by" stories suggests about the stories we tell ourselves. What does it mean when a story is "inspired by" rather than "based upon" a true event? How should we understand these types of stories when we encounter them in the real world?

Process (5 minutes):

When selecting photos, consider choosing a variety of images from around the region or the world. An ideal photo for this activity is one that includes a number of interesting visual details, but that is ambiguous enough that, even with the caption, viewers may have difficulty determining what exactly they are looking at.

Provide students with copies of the news photos you selected for this activity. Decide in advance if you want all students writing about the same photo, if you want to assign different Teams different photos, or if you want to have students move around the room to find their own inspiration photo from a gallery wall you post while students are drafting during the anticipatory activity. Provide students with five minutes to explore their photos in detail and begin brainstorming a narrative.

Figure 4.1 Students exploring their *Inspired by a True Story* photos (screen images deliberately blurred)

Drafting (30 minutes):

Students will now draft for 30 minutes, being sure to start their draft with the words: "The following was inspired by a true story . . . " Using any of the details they observed in their inspiration photo, they are to write a story connected to that image.

Writing Team Share (25 minutes):
Have students share their stories with their Writing Team. As they share, they should begin with the words, "The following was inspired by a true story." Depending on the photo process you selected, ask the Writing Team to either identify the photo the student was working with or the details from the photo they picked up on as the primary inspiration for their story. Each member of the Writing Team should share their stories before moving on to the reflection stage.

Reflection (10 minutes):
As a closing activity, ask students to reflect in their Writer's Notebook about the process for today's activity. Provide them with the full details that accompany their photo (for example, a copy of the article the photo was connected to) so they have a sense of the real story.

- How did the details they selected from the photo shape their narrative?

- How similar or dissimilar was their story from the story of others who were working with the same photo?

- How similar or dissimilar was their story from the actual event that inspired it?

- How did the inclusion of the words "The following was inspired by a true story" affect their initial response to and/or interpretation of the narrative?

- What does this suggest about the effect of this language when added to other narratives we encounter in real-life?

Differentiate

To Support:
To reinforce the goals of this particular activity for younger/struggling learners, assign all members of each Writing Team a common photo. However, each student in the group can be asked to focus on a different detail from the source photo as their inspiration (or even a different quadrant of the photo). After they write and share, they will realize the role that their choice of focus played in shaping their narratives, thus reinforcing the idea that "inspired by" and "based upon" a true story are very different frameworks.

To Challenge:
To challenge advanced learners, consider adding in a layer of complexity to their writing prompt. Rather than simply asking them to develop a narrative inspired by the photo, ask them to begin by writing with a purpose—for example, to anger the audience, to make the audience cheer for the photo's subject, to inform, etc. Then, as their drafting time continues, interrupt them periodically to force new details into their story. For example, they can be forced to narrow their focus on a particular quadrant of the image, an item visible in the background, etc.

Suggested Unit Integration:
There are a wide variety of ways this lesson could be incorporated into a larger instructional framework. Below are a few suggestions:

- *Visual Media:* Incorporate this lesson into a nonfiction unit that includes an exploration of visual media. For example, if you wanted to integrate this activity into your larger instructional unit, you may spend some of your instructional days comparing and contrasting photos from two opposing news sources that feature the same event and consider how the selection of photos and details shapes the readers' understanding of events.

- *Selection of Details:* When we teach students to analyze literature, we ask them to provide evidence to support their findings. The key to success with this task is ensuring that students understand how the selection of details supports (or can undermine) their argument. For this integration activity, provide students with a nonfiction news article and a variety of possible photos to include alongside it. As part of the instructional lesson, students should be asked to select which photo to add to the news article and explain their choice, being sure to consider how the rhetorical situation from the article informed their selection.

- *Global Perspectives:* Pair this activity with a lesson on global perspectives by following the same news story in newspapers around the world and then consider how perspective informs or shapes our perception of our world.

- *Nonfiction vs. Fiction:* Embed this lesson into a larger nonfiction unit that involves students reading nonfiction accounts of an event from history as well as fictionalized interpretations of that event. For example, you may wish to pair a reading of Elie Wiesel's memoir, *Night,* with paired excerpts from Markus Zusak's novel, *The Book Thief,* or nonfiction news accounts of the Cambodian Genocide with Vaddey Ratner's novel, *In the Shadow of the Banyan.* Then, ask students to consider the difference between nonfiction and fiction and the effect of each genre on their understanding of historical events.

Extension Activity:

- *Self-Reflective Comparative Analysis:* Ask students to source an image from their photo library. Then, they should write the story of that photo in two ways: one to reflect a story that is based on actual events and one to reflect a story that is inspired by actual events. As part of the assignment, they should be asked to write a reflection that compares and contrasts how the story changes when it is "based upon" versus when it is "inspired by" true events.

- *Nonfiction/Research Comparative Analysis:* Provide students with an image from history. Then, ask them to research that event and write a story two ways: once to reflect the story that is based on actual events and once to reflect a story that is inspired by actual events. As part of the assignment, students should be asked to write a reflection that considers the effect of depicting events in a nonfiction versus fictionalized manner. This extension activity

would pair very well with the "Nonfiction vs. Fiction" Unit Integration activity suggested above.

- *Visual Media:* Ask students to develop a photo essay based either on a particular real-world event, a whole-class fictional reading, or their own lives. How does creating an essay composed primarily of visual texts differ from a written essay? What are the advantages and disadvantages of each type of media? How can the knowledge gleaned from this activity shape their understanding of rhetorical contexts and authorial choices when developing future creation tasks? (See **Figure 4.2** for sample instructions for this extension activity.)

Figure 4.2

Extension Activity: Literary Analysis Using Visual Media

Directions: For this activity, you will be developing a literary analysis piece—with a twist. Rather than developing a standard essay, this activity requires you to develop a photo essay in which you help your reader reach an understanding of the text through the skillful incorporation of both written and visual elements.

First, select from one of the prompts below, being sure to explore the significance of your findings as part of your response:

- **Majorly Minor:** Select the one minor character from your text who you believe has the most impact on the development of the larger narrative. Then, develop an argument in which you support your findings using textual evidence.

- **Cause and Effect:** Consider your story in light of its literary conflicts. Then, develop an argument in which you show which elements of the text serve as the catalyst (the cause) for one or more of these conflicts, being sure to consider whether you want your reader to understand more about the cause or the effect as part of your argument.

- **Where it all Went Down:** Explore one or more of the settings in your text. Then, develop an argument in which you explore how the author uses setting to shape the larger narrative.

- **Before and After:** Select one of the dynamic characters from your text. Then, develop an argument in which you explore how one or more moments or events from the story serves to transform that character.

Figure 4.2 continued

Once you have selected your prompt, it is time to develop your photo essay. Your final product should include no fewer than three visual images that serve to reflect and/or support the claims you are making in your written argument. Remember to consider your rhetorical situation when developing your product. Consider:

➤ What is my rhetorical goal and how does that inform my choices?

➤ Who is my audience and how does that affect my approach including tone, voice, and text-to-image ratio?

➤ How will I use visual media to support my goal?

   o What types of images will best support my larger argument?

   o What rhetorical voice(s) should I employ: ethos, pathos, logos?

   o Where in the document shall I include my images and why?

➤ How will my written and visual elements work together to support my goal?

Reflection: As part of your submission, be sure to include a written reflection that explains the choices you made while drafting and the reasons why you made those choices. You may wish to reflect upon the bulleted questions above to guide your reflection. Be sure to provide specific evidence from your finished product to support your rationale.

Killing Time
Prep Time: High

Description:

This activity, like its partner lesson, *Making Time*, challenges students to control the pace of their writing through strategic narrative choices. Whereas *Making Time* teaches students to slow time down through elaboration and selection of detail, *Killing Time* teaches students to speed up the pace of their writing by condensing the narrative to its smallest components. In this lesson, students will explore how to condense their writing through careful selection of detail, strategic word choice, and syntax structure. They will first condense a sample passage for practice before exploring one of their own creative pieces in which they want to "kill time."

Student-Friendly Objectives:	*Materials:*
By the end of this lesson, students will be able to: <ul><li>Consider and select the most critical elements necessary to drive their narrative goals</li><li>Adjust content, diction, and syntax to control the pace of their writing</li></ul>	<ul><li>Sample paired excerpts from the same text—one where the passage is rich with elaborative details and the narrative pace slows and one where the focus is extremely narrow and the narrative pace increases</li></ul>

Rationale:

Both teachers and students often focus on content above style when it comes to writing instruction, and for understandable reasons. However, stylistic choices are an important component of quality writing, not only because style makes a text more approachable and, therefore, more likely to achieve a Writer's goals, but also because style involves many of the same critical thinking skills that content considerations require. As with content creation, Writers must carefully consider their writing goals and their audience when determining how best to approach their draft from a stylistic perspective. In a similar fashion, they must make strategic choices about what details to include, what word choices are most appropriate, and how to arrange their sentences to control the reader's experience with the text.

Making strategic choices about where to speed the reader up or slow them down has consequences for what details the reader will focus on and, in turn, how they come to understand the text. Therefore, emphasizing to students that both content and style are important considerations when drafting a text will ensure that they are making strategic choices not only of what they will say, but how they will say it.

Anticipatory Activity (15 minutes):
Place students into their Writing Teams and provide each Team with a small packet of sample passages from the same text. Within the packet, ensure that at least one of the excerpts features elaborative details that slow the reader down and one excerpt where the writing is condensed with the effect of speeding the reader up.

In their Writing Teams, members should compare and contrast the provided excerpts, taking notes in the Observation section of their Writer's Notebook. For younger/struggling students, you may wish to give them a focus for their exploration—in this case, pacing. For older students or students who are ready for a challenge, be deliberately vague about their reading focus and see if any of the Teams instinctively pick up on the differences in style, as opposed to differences in content.

Lead a brief whole-class discussion where Teams explain their observations. Moderate the discussion to both keep it brief and ensure that some discussion of style is included before moving on to the next stage.

Process (30 minutes):
Students now move around to various Rotation Stations set up around the room. At each station, place a set of paired passages from the same text, one that is slower and more elaborative and one that moves the reader more quickly through time. Make sure to include a variety of authors, writing styles, and genres. Be careful also to select passages where the technique the author uses to "kill time" differs. For example, some authors kill time through the strategic use of alternating dialogue

If you choose to be vague about the reading purpose for the anticipatory activity, selecting paired passages where the content is relatively similar will increase the chances that students will instinctively pick up on the style contrasts. If the focus of each passage is too dissimilar, students will most likely default to a comparative exploration of content rather than style.

where there is no elaboration before or after the dialogue shifts (i.e., the dialogue moves in rapid-fire progression rather than slowing down with "he said," "she rolled her eyes," etc.) Other authors kill time through the use of extremely short sentences or small one- or two-sentence paragraphs. Still others speed time with the repeated use of short monosyllabic words. Make sure that each Rotation Station brings something new to students' understanding of how to "kill time" so they understand the breadth of stylistic choices they can employ when crafting their own writing.

Suggest that students rotate to no fewer than three stations as they conduct their exploration. At each, they should read the paired passages (keep these passages fairly short—perhaps fitting each one in a side-by-side column for easy and quick comparison) and take notes about the author's technique in the Observation section of their Writer's Notebook.

Figure 4.3 provides sample questions for students to consider during this stage of the activity.

Figure 4.3

Observation Questions

❖ What details did the author choose to elaborate upon in the slower-paced passage?

❖ What details got included in the faster-paced passage? Excluded?

❖ What technique(s) did the author utilize to control pacing in each passage? For example:

- Dialogue
- Syntax (sentence structure)
- Paragraph/content breaks
- Diction (word choice)
- Punctuation

Drafting (20 minutes):
Students should now spend twenty minutes reviewing their Writer's Notebook and selecting one draft that they would like to revise to incorporate condensed writing. Once they have selected their draft, they should determine where in the text they feel the story would benefit from some speeding up. Do they want to completely rewrite an existing passage to speed up the pace? Do they want to layer in a new passage mid-way through their writing to speed up time? Do they want to add some new passages at the beginning or end of the draft to speed things up? Why? How will they achieve their desired effect (i.e., what stylistic techniques will they use to "kill time")? Once they have brainstormed their changes, they should use their remaining drafting time to begin the revision process.

Writing Team Share (20 minutes):
At the end of their drafting time, students should share their work with their Writing Team being sure to include a discussion of why they selected that particular draft, how they determined where they wanted to kill time, and what stylistic techniques they employed to achieve their desired effect. Once all members have had a chance to share, Teams should discuss the various different techniques employed by the group members and how each technique shaped the overall narrative.

Reflection (5 minutes):
Students spend the final five minutes of class reflecting on the process of "killing time" in their Writer's Notebook.

- What did they learn about how and why to control the pacing of their writing to achieve the desired effect?

- What are the application possibilities for both fiction and nonfiction writing?

- How might they be able to use this knowledge when crafting their own writing in the future?

Differentiate

To Support:

As suggested in the anticipatory activity instructions, support younger/struggling learners by providing them a focus for reading when conducting the opening activity. This relieves some of the pressure by giving them guidance on what they should be looking for as they explore the first paired passage and will allow them to feel more confident when it comes time for the whole-class discussion that follows.

When students move to the Rotation Stations, provide a graphic organizer that highlights each of the pacing techniques your samples employ (for example: dialogue, syntax, word choice). Have students indicate which texts employ each technique to reinforce their understanding of the skill. Finally, consider turning the Rotation Station activity into a Writing Team game where Teams compete to correctly find and match each passage to its stylistic approach. Turning this portion of the activity into a game makes the activity feel more comfortable. Turning it into a collaborative game helps better support students by allowing them to work and brainstorm together.

To Challenge:

Challenge students by requiring them to revise their drafts by including two or more different stylistic techniques to control pacing in their revision pieces. They can accomplish this goal either by employing two different techniques in one draft, or they can revise multiple drafts to incorporate a different approach in each one. They should be asked to explain their choices to their Writing Team when they share and again in their Reflection piece.

Suggested Unit Integration:

Pair this activity with short stories you have read before this activity. Include a wide array of short stories from a variety of authors that span diverse genres. Then, adapt this activity so that rather than revising one of their own creative pieces, students outline the main events from one or more of these short stories and then convert those events into an even shorter narrative such as a vignette that captures either the essence of the entire story or a key moment from that story.

Extension Activity:

- *Multimedia Project:* Working with either a short story or a longer whole-class text, ask students to create a video movie trailer which, like any good movie trailer, features short bursts of content that, when assembled together, serve to tell a story (or allow the viewer to infer what the story is about).

- *Publication Piece:* After students have completed both this activity and its partner lesson, *Making Time*, ask students to develop an original narrative that features areas where the text both slows down and speeds up in a way that is designed to deliberately, and meaningfully, control the reader's pace, thus affecting their understanding of the text as a whole. As part of this assignment, students should include a rationale explaining their choices.

- *Researching Authentic Uses:* Ask students to work collaboratively to research and present about communication modes that feature short bursts of content (e.g., movie trailers, performance videos, blogs, commercials, elevator pitches, etc.). Then, they should select one to research in more detail, exploring the key features of that genre including when and how that genre can be used to deliver effective communication (see **Figure 4.4** for sample instructions for this extension activity).

Figure 4.4

Extension Activity: Researching Authentic Uses

Directions: Work with your Writing Team to research one of the following short communication forms:

- Movie Trailers
- Book Blurbs (the content on the back of a book or inside the dust jacket)
- Tweets
- Emails
- Commercials
- Tik Toks
- Elevator Pitches
- Blogs
- Cover Letters
- College Application Essays

Then, develop a multimedia presentation in which you explore (in any order):

- ❏ The history/origins of your selected form and its purpose
- ❏ Key conventions of your selected form
- ❏ At least three high-quality examples of your selected form in use
- ❏ Best practices for how/when to use your selected form
- ❏ Advantages and limitations of your selected form

Be sure to include proper citations for your research sources and example texts.

Musical Muses
Prep Time: Medium

Description:

This activity focuses students' attention on developing tone and mood through their writing choices. In this lesson, students explore an artistic genre they are almost universally familiar with—music—and consider how musical elements can inspire their own written creations. Students will gain inspiration from a selected piece of music and, based on their evaluation of tone, mood, and pacing, will craft an original narrative that reflects their inspiration song.

Student-Friendly Objectives:	*Materials:*
By the end of this lesson, students will be able to: • Consider and select the most critical elements necessary to drive their narrative goals • Adjust their writing to achieve their desired tonal and rhythmic effect	• Samples of music representing different styles and genres but focused on a common theme or sets of themes • Sample artwork placed around the room for additional inspiration (optional) • Headphones for each student (optional but strongly recommended)

Rationale:

The literary world is full of examples of authors incorporating music directly or indirectly into their own writing. For example, John Steinbeck famously sought inspiration from the score to *Swan Lake* when writing *The Grapes of Wrath*, and Ralph Waldo Ellison embedded musical elements directly into his novel, *Invisible Man*. Ann Patchett and Keiichiro Hirano wrote entire novels focused on musicians. Students themselves often complain that they cannot work unless they have music playing softly in the background. Music is, indeed, one of the most universally understood and adored modes of communication, and while not everyone agrees on their preferred musical genre, it's hard to find anyone who does not like any music at all. Therefore, this activity taps into students' own cultural identities to demonstrate the connection between music and the written word to enhance their understanding of how literary and stylistic choices affect meaning.

If you have students with auditory concerns, make sure that you consider how best to support their learning when implementing this lesson into your own classes.

119

Anticipatory Activity (15 minutes):
Once students are settled at their desks, ask them to write for five minutes in their Writer's Notebook in connection with a theme topic you provide. The direction they take when responding to that topic is entirely up to them. Once five minutes have passed, ask for a few volunteers to quickly discuss the direction they took as they explored this topic.

Then, play a minute or two of several songs that explore your selected topic. **Figure 4.5** provides an example of what this activity might look like in your classroom.

Figure 4.5

Anticipatory Activity

The content below is provided for illustrative purposes only. In your own classes, the theme topic and paired songs you select should be adjusted to reflect your instructional needs and the music you select should be used with appropriate permissions.

Theme Topic	Sample Songs	Why These Songs Work
Mistakes	Sarah McLachlan's "Fallen" Metallica's "Unforgiven" Louis Armstrong's "Black and Blue"	Each of these songs deals with a different element of mistakes: resignation, forgiveness (or lack thereof), and confusion. In addition, each song features a wildly different tone, mood, and genre.

Play enough of each song that students are able to hold a brief, but informed, discussion on how the tone/mood of the music connects to the theme topic and how the tone/mood and theme work together to develop an understanding of meaning. For example, a student might observe that the somber tone and slow pace of McLachlan's "Fallen," helps develop a mood of sorrow and resignation.

Process (25 minutes):

Have students wander to different Rotation Stations situated around the room. Each station should feature a set of songs focused around a shared theme topic. Like the anticipatory activity, the songs you select should showcase diverse approaches to and interpretations of the theme topic in question. As they move to the various stations, students should take notes in the Observation section of their Writer's Notebook. See **Figure 4.6** for sample instructions for this stage of the lesson.

Once students have made their way to several of the stations, allow students to select one of the theme topics they would like to explore further. Then, have them select one song from any of the Rotation Stations they visited to serve as inspiration for the tone and mood of their own original narrative.

Although it may be tempting to create a playlist on your class webpage for students to access from their desks, doing so may inadvertently result in copyright infringement. Whenever you are using protected material for instructional purposes in your classes, be sure you are doing so with appropriate permissions.

Figure 4.6

Observation Instructions

Directions: For each of the stations you visit, add an entry to the Observation section of your Writer's Notebook that responds to the prompts below. You should visit no fewer than three stations during this portion of the activity.

Station Theme Topic:

Real-World Connotation of this Theme Topic:

    ___ Positive   ___ Negative   ___ Neutral

Song 1 Title & Artist:

Tone:

Mood:

Pacing:

Connotative Treatment of the Theme Topic Within the Song:

    ___ Positive   ___ Negative   ___ Neutral

What this song reveals about the nature of its associated theme topic:

Examples from the song that support your findings:

Artfulness

Using their observations, students should develop a creative narrative that addresses their chosen theme topic while employing a tone and mood similar to the one featured in their chosen song. If you feel students may need some additional inspiration as a story starter, consider posting visual images around the room for them to wander to for additional inspiration. A mixture of painted art, photography, architecture, landscapes, even some textural elements to physically touch may provide them with sufficient inspiration for the subject of their writing.

Drafting (35 minutes):
Students should spend thirty-five minutes drafting their narrative, making sure that their narrative reflects a similar tone and mood to the inspiration song. As they draft, they should review their observations regularly and adjust their writing to better reflect their selected song. For example, if the tone and mood changes as the song progresses, they should adjust the tone and mood of their own narrative to reflect that shift. Students should have enough to keep them busy for the full thirty-five minutes. However, if you have early finishers, ask them to adjust their writing to reflect the relative length of their inspiration song. For example, if their song was relatively short, ask them to revise their story to make it more concise. If their song was relatively long, ask them to elaborate to reflect the length of the song.

Writing Team Share (15 minutes):
Students close out today's lesson by sharing their work while playing a portion of their selected song. In this manner, Writing Teams will be able to hear the tone and mood of the piece clearly and identify the connections the writer made between their inspiration piece and their own original narrative. As part of their share, students should briefly discuss their writing process to explain the choices they made.

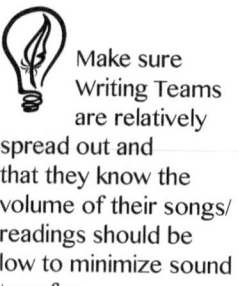
Make sure Writing Teams are relatively spread out and that they know the volume of their songs/readings should be low to minimize sound transfer.

122

Differentiate

To Support:

Because this activity involves a fair amount of audio, pay particular attention to the needs of students who have auditory concerns such as those with hearing impairments, sound sensitivities, and students who may be concussed. Be sure to provide differentiated experiences for those learners so that their needs are properly supported.

For younger/struggling learners, provide a graphic organizer that helps them explore the tone and mood of the piece so they have a clearer sense of what to capture in their own writing. Consider having them listen to the song twice during this process—once to take notes on elements of the song that establish tone and mood, and once to take notes on where in the song the various tones and/or moods are developed or shifted.

To Challenge:

You can easily increase or decrease the challenge with this activity through your selection of song options. To increase the rigor, select complex songs that incorporate considerable shifts in tone and mood.

Enhance students' critical thinking skills further by requiring them to match one of the songs to one of the inspiration art pieces around the room and to justify their choices in a written reflection at the end of the activity.

Suggested Unit Integration:

Pair this activity with close reading explorations of written passages. Spend a few days exploring a handful of passages from a variety of texts and consider how the author uses diction, syntax, and other stylistic choices both to develop tone and mood and to create meaning. To align with this activity, focus your close reading evaluation specifically on diction and style, expanding as appropriate to a consideration of how syntax affects tone and mood as well. If your students are ready for a challenge, this can be a great opportunity to discuss syntax and grammar choices such as asyndeton and polysyndeton, commas/colons/semicolons, and clauses.

Artfulness

Extension Activity:

- *Literary Analysis:* Combine this lesson with poetry readings or close readings of musically rich texts. Then, ask students to write a literary analysis essay that explores how the author uses stylistic elements such as diction, syntax, and rhythm to shape the work as a whole.

- *Publication Piece/Oral Presentation:* Ask students to revise and finalize their draft so that it represents a complete narrative that aligns with their selected song. Then, ask them to record themselves reading their draft with the music playing in the background so that the listener can hear the connection between their narrative and their selected song.

- *Research—Authentic Connections:* Ask students to research music in their everyday lives. The choices here are endless: What does the science say about music and focus? What types of music do plants best respond to and why? What are some of the earliest musical instruments known to mankind? What is the connection between music and storytelling?

- *Research—Creative Connections:* Have students research authors who were known to have employed music directly into their writing. What is the background of these authors and how does their background impact their writing? What stylistic approaches did they employ to incorporate a sense of musicality in their writing? What passages from their writing best exemplify their particular technique? See **Figure 4.7** for sample instructions for this extension activity.

- *Vocabulary:* If you elect to pair this activity with a lesson on grammar, have students update their Technical Vocabulary list to capture any new terminology or new understandings of previously studied terminology.

Figure 4.7

Extension Activity: Researching Creative Connections

The connection between song lyrics and poetry has long been recognized. But the relationship between music and storytelling goes much deeper than that. For this assignment, you will research a major musical style or movement and create a multimedia presentation in which you explore how this musical style or movement has shaped (or been shaped by) the written word.

Here are some ideas to get you started. If you would like to suggest your own musical style or movement, please schedule a conference with me to discuss your vision.

Alternative Rock	Ballads	Bluegrass	Broadway Musicals
Choral Odes	Classical Music	Country Western	Disco
Go-Go	Gospel Music	Hip Hop	Jazz
Rhythm & Blues	Opera	Rap	Rock

Requirements: Your presentation should include a meaningful exploration of the following:

❖ The origins and history of your musical genre

❖ Key conventions of this musical genre

❖ The connection between this genre and storytelling, complete with examples

❖ How this musical genre shaped or was shaped by storytelling elements, complete with relevant examples to support your findings

❖ Famous works/musicians associated with this musical genre

❖ The role of this musical genre in the modern world

❖ Proper source citations

Numbers
Prep Time: Low

Description:

Inspired by a game on Food Network's television show, "Guy's Grocery Games," in this lesson, students will be given a set of number cards and a writing prompt. Students are then given a set of literary elements (the same number of literary elements as there are number cards) that they must include in their creative writing product. Each student will assign one of the number cards to a corresponding literary element. They should repeat this process until all of the number cards have been matched to a corresponding literary element, and they cannot use a number card more than once. For example, if you provide number cards 2, 3, and 5 to students and then require them to incorporate setting, character, and metaphor, they must decide how many of each required element they have to weave into their story by assigning one of their number cards to a corresponding literary element. Then, they must create a draft narrative in which they force the corresponding number of each element into the text in a cohesive and unified way.

Figure 4.8

Set Up

To set up this activity, determine which literary elements you would like your students to work with and the number value options you would like to provide. Then, ask each student to match their desired number value to those elements. For example:

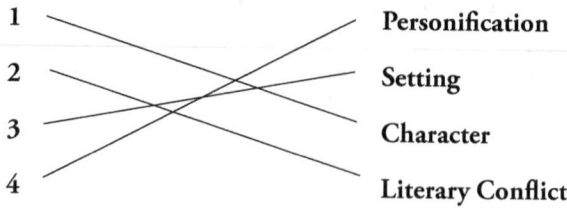

Student-Friendly Objectives:
By the end of this lesson, students will be able to:

- Incorporate a variety of literary elements into their own original narratives
- Make thoughtful choices about how best to incorporate literary elements into their own writing

Materials:

- Set of number cards for each student

 You can save resources by writing each number and literary element on the board and having students indicate their selections in their Writer's Notebook as an alternative to using number cards for this activity.

Rationale:

In order to scaffold instruction well, when we teach literary elements, we often focus on one discrete element at a time—character, setting, POV, etc. While this is an effective technique when introducing literary elements, if we stop at this stage, we may inadvertently leave students with the impression that literary elements work in isolation from one another—that we can evaluate the author's use of setting, for example, without fully considering how that setting connects to the larger narrative. This lesson addresses that effect by forcing students to build their own cohesive narrative using a variety, both in number and in type, of literary elements.

Because they have to grapple with how to incorporate literary elements such as multiple settings and an internal conflict into one unified story, students come to realize the thoughtfulness that goes into each authorial choice and how each individual choice an author makes affects the larger narrative. It is through the process of construction that students begin to appreciate the interconnectedness of literary elements and techniques. This lesson, therefore, enhances not only their ability to write effectively, but also their ability to analyze the writing of others effectively.

*Artfulness*

This lesson provides a great opportunity to integrate cross-curricular skills. Speak to teachers in the other academic departments before finalizing your lessons plans to see what lessons and units they are currently studying.. For example, if your students are currently learning about the Industrial Revolution in history class, develop story prompts that would allow them to produce historical fiction focused on that time period.

Process (5 minutes):

Provide each student with a set of number cards and literary elements in the quantity you desire. Make sure there are an equal number of number cards and literary elements. Then, provide the writing prompt you would like students to work with. For example: "Today you are going to write a fantasy short story set in 2347," or "You are going to write about a woman with a dangerous secret who has arrived at a crossroad."

Tell students that they are required to use each of the literary elements with which they have been provided. You can adjust the challenge here by selecting more foundational or more elevated literary elements as appropriate for your student body. However, I recommend working with literary elements you are confident your students already know.

Next, ask students to match each number card to their desired literary element but warn them that once they assign that element a number, they must incorporate a corresponding number of that literary element into their narrative. For example, if they assign the number four to a "narrative perspective" card, they must change the narrative perspective four times during the course of their writing.

Drafting (60 minutes):

Provide sixty minutes for students to complete their drafting. They should be writing for the entire time. If you find that your students lose focus with a lengthy drafting time, consider modifying this lesson so that you add more required elements that they have to weave in once their writing is already underway. Giving these new elements a playful name like "curve balls" or "twists" helps to keep the addition of these elements fun. Keep in mind, however, that adding other required elements in this manner does increase the challenge level a bit.

In the final two or three minutes, let students know that time is winding down so they have a chance to begin moving towards a purposeful ending.

Writing Team Share (15 minutes):

Students will share their drafts with their Writing Team, being sure to tell their Team members how they matched their elements. After they share, students should discuss with their Team what they felt worked well and ask for guidance on how to address any areas they feel need additional attention.

Reflection (10 minutes):
After the share, students will reflect in their Writer's Notebook about the process of forcing multiple quantities of literary elements into one narrative.

- What did they learn about how literary elements and techniques work together to shape a narrative?

- How might they use their new understanding when reading and evaluating the works of others?

Differentiate

To Support:	*To Challenge:*
Support younger/struggling learners by selecting more foundational literary elements for them to incorporate into this activity and using relatively low number cards to avoid overwhelming them. You may also wish to spend an instructional day or two before this lesson exploring short stories and excerpts of longer fiction that contain multiple conflicts, characters, lines of dialogue, setting, narrative perspectives, etc. (whatever elements you are planning on using in this activity), and having students annotate and evaluate how the literary elements you are exploring work together to shape the narrative. This will provide some foundational knowledge for students to tap into during their writing time.	Increase the challenge of this activity by providing higher number cards and/or selecting more advanced literary elements such as multiple time periods, narrative perspectives, higher-level figurative devices, lines of dialogue, etc. You can increase the rigor further by revealing each literary device one at a time so that students have to match a number to the first literary element without knowing in advance what other literary elements they will be required to incorporate later. Alternatively, turn this activity into a competition by having different Writing Teams assign the numbers and elements to a rival Team.

Artfulness

Suggested Unit Integration:

- *Younger Students:* Incorporate this lesson near the end of a unit in which you explore literary elements such as character, setting, POV, etc. Once students have had a chance to gain experience evaluating an author's use of each device in isolation, they will be ready to extend their understanding of how literary elements work together to shape a unified text. After students have had a chance to grapple with how to incorporate a variety of literary elements together into one narrative, they will be better equipped to evaluate how the authors of their whole-class texts use these elements together to shape meaning.

- *Older Students:* Pair this activity with more advanced and/or challenging texts that incorporate, for example, multiple time periods, multiple narrative perspectives, complex portrayals of characters, or ideas that are linked meaningfully to other literary elements such as setting or symbols. In the days leading up to this activity, ask students to draft a literary analysis essay that explores how the author of their whole-class text uses literary elements to shape meaning. Then, conduct this activity. In the instructional days after this activity, ask students to revisit their first draft and revise their argument based on their new understanding of how the author uses literary elements to shape meaning. Ask them to attach a reflection that documents how their understanding evolved after attempting their own multi-element narrative.

Extension Activity:

- *Nonfiction:* Follow this activity with a reading of a narrative nonfiction text. Using the knowledge gained from this experience, have students annotate and evaluate how nonfiction authors incorporate a variety of narrative elements to weave engaging nonfiction tales. Then, have students select one of their nonfiction reports they may have written for another class such as a history or a science report, and revise that writing to incorporate narrative elements that may appeal to the general reading public.

- *Student-Curated Mentor Texts:* Provide students with the same number cards and literary elements used when completing this lesson but this time, require students to explore their own readings to find the designated number of each literary element. For each example they find, they must write that example (either a direct quote or a detailed summary, as appropriate), the name of the text, author from which they sourced the example, the page number where the example can be found, and a brief analytical exploration of how that example functions in that particular context (see **Figure 4.9** for sample instructions for this extension activity).

- *Vocabulary:* Have students add to or revise their Technical Vocabulary word list to reflect their new understanding for each term studied as part of this lesson.

Figure 4.9

Extension Activity: Student-Curated Mentor Texts

Directions: Using the number cards and literary elements explored during our *Numbers* lesson, you should now explore your own readings to source quality examples of the literary elements we worked with in class. For each literary element, source the same number of examples as the number you included in your own original narrative. For example, if you included three characters in your narrative, you should find three examples of quality characterization in your own readings.

Each entry should include:

- ☐ The name of the literary element being explored
- ☐ The title and author of your source text
- ☐ A quote or detailed summary that provides a clear example of that element in use, along with the page number(s) where this element can be found in the text, and
- ☐ A brief (three to five sentence) analysis of how that literary element functions in that context to shape meaning

---

Mashup
Prep Time: High

Description:

In this lesson, students will explore musical mashups to inspire them to create their own literary mashups using whole-class texts or sample texts provided by the teacher. Rather than producing an original narrative of their own, they will experiment with blending to see how they can combine works of others to create a new interpretation of that work.

Before class starts, arrange these texts around the room in Rotation Stations. Have multiple copies of each Rotation Station text available for students to bring back to their desks while they draft.

Student-Friendly Objectives:
By the end of this lesson, students will be able to:

- Compare and contrast two or more literary texts to find areas of harmony between them
- Select the details and elements from each text that will be most effective in creating the desired harmonious effect

Materials:

- Video clips of sample musical mashups (these are easily sourced with a simple online search—be careful to preview all video selections to ensure they are appropriate for your classes)
- A variety of literary texts drawn either from the broader whole-class reading units or selected by the teacher specifically for this activity

Rationale:

While one could argue that a mashup is, by definition, derivative, rather than creative, the process of seeking out areas of harmony across texts is an important skill for students to master. This activity teaches students to explore texts in conversation and promotes the development of synthesis skills. In addition, as students seek to explore how diverse texts can work together, we are challenging students to read both closely and critically, further developing their literary analysis skills in the process of this creation task.

Anticipatory Activity (10 minutes):

As a whole class, watch the sample musical mashup you selected for today's activity. As they watch, students should be taking notes in the

Observation section of their Writer's Notebook. If they recognize what songs are being mashed together, they may wish to write them down along with the musical genre, if known. They should also note what elements are mashed together (for example, the background music of one song with the lyrics of another, the words from different songs blended together, blended harmonies, etc.) and any other pertinent observations they may notice. If you are concerned students may not be familiar with the mashup songs, play each one first as a stand-alone song before showcasing the mashup video. If you take that approach, be sure to adjust the suggested timeframe for this activity accordingly so you don't run out of time later in the class.

Once students have had a chance to observe the video and process their observations, ask for two or three volunteers to share their observations.

Process (15 minutes):
Next, students move around to the Rotation Stations to explore their text options. Depending on instructional needs, you may wish to organize the stations by theme, genre, essential question, or some other literary element connected to your broader instruction. You can easily control the amount of student choice involved based on how you design the Rotation Stations.

Drafting (45 minutes):
Since students will need to copy selected excerpts from each of their chosen texts verbatim, they should bring a copy of their selected texts back to their desks to work. Then, students begin the process of mashing the two (or more) texts together into a unified, cohesive new narrative. Their new narrative should use only the words of the original authors, with extremely minimal additions permitted (such as the addition of a preposition or a pronoun) to allow for appropriate transitions between ideas.

 Depending on student needs, you may wish to break this activity into two days and spend one day having students explore a variety of different mashups at Rotation Stations and then working together to reflect on their learning before moving into the creative stage on Day 2. This scaffold will provide more time for students to understand the variety of structural options they have when creating their own work.

 *Artfulness*

Writing Team Share (10 minutes):
Once they have completed their drafts, each student should share their creation with their Writing Team. Reading their work aloud will enable students to instantly hear if any of the text fusings didn't quite align. As they read, students should use different color ink to note any outstanding technical edits they need to make to correct blending issues.

Reflection (10 minutes):
After all members of the Writing Team have shared their creations and made note of any needed revisions, individual students should write a reflection that asks them to explain their choices:

- What texts did they select for this activity and why?

- What areas of harmony did they observe across the texts and how did these harmonious elements affect what portions of each text they selected to fuse together?

- What was the most difficult/challenging part of this process?

- How satisfied are they with their current draft? What are they most proud of? What would they like to revise?

- How did this process affect the way they evaluate texts and, in particular, how they compare and contrast texts in conversation?

Differentiate

To Support:	*To Challenge:*
To support younger/struggling learners, spread this lesson out over two days. On Day 1, place students into their Writing Teams and have them listen to each of the original songs from the mashup in its entirety. For each song, ask the group to capture their observations about the original song—what theme topic does the song address, what is the pacing like, the rhythm, the tone, etc.? Then, provide students with the mashup version of the songs. Using a graphic organizer, Teams should explore the mashup to analyze how the new version of the song is assembled. What elements did the creator of the mashup seek to highlight (i.e., what areas of harmony did they find between/across songs)? Did they blend the lyrics together, or overlap the lyrics from one song over the harmony of the other, etc.?	Ask students to mashup three or more texts into one cohesive whole.

Increase the challenge further by asking students to write their mashup in a particular genre (e.g., poem for two voices, drama, satirical monologue, etc.) or challenge them to showcase a particular literary element such as characterization or irony with their mashup. |

Suggested Unit Integration:

Pair this lesson with any fiction or nonfiction unit you are currently teaching or have previously taught to your students. For example, if you are reading a whole-class text together and you have been providing paired supplemental readings (fiction, nonfiction, poetry, etc.), you can pull from any or all of those texts for students to work with during this activity. You can enhance this integration suggestion further by pulling from *all* of the texts you have worked with in your class so far. This would challenge students to conduct deeper, more thoughtful synthesis by asking them to reconsider both current and previous units as units in conversation. For students who need more scaffolds, offer an Essential Question or a theme topic for them to consider when they revisit all of these texts. For students who are ready for a challenge, simply provide copies of your chosen excerpts and allow their imaginations to take over.

Artfulness

Extension Activity:

- *Comparative Analysis:* Provide students with an Essential Question and then ask them to write a comparative analysis that explores how each text works together to answer that question, being sure to cite evidence from both texts in support of their findings.

- *Literary Analysis:* Ask students to explore foil characters in one of your readings. Then, have them create a character mashup wherein they take dialogue or narration connected to both characters and blend these text elements together so that they create a narrative that depicts these foils as one cohesive character (see **Figure 4.10** on page 137 for sample instructions for this extension activity).

- *Multimedia Project:* Ask students to convert their literary mashup into a multimedia product in the form of a music video, a short film, a comic strip, or similar. As part of their submission, students should include a reflection that explores the choices they made and how those choices worked to enhance the effectiveness of their piece.

- *Synthesis Research:* Extend student learning by requiring students to curate their own texts-in-conversation set that responds to an Essential Question or that speaks to a shared theme topic. Their final product should take the format of a formal research essay, complete with proper citations, that includes evidence pulled from the complete text set they assembled.

QUARTER 3 CELEBRATION DAY

Congratulations on reaching the end of the third quarter. The end of the year is rapidly approaching and students should be growing comfortable stretching their creative wings.

Although students have been challenged to integrate a range of skills and techniques in their writing this quarter, the emphasis of most lessons has been style, style, style. The Quarter 3 Celebration Day, therefore, requires students to make thoughtful and deliberate style choices that are designed to create a sense of musicality in their writing. Anchoring their Team Showcase on a true story that inspired their work, students must find ways to harmonize their own individual writing vision with that of their teammates to create a cohesive, unified Team product.

Figure 4.10 from page 136

Extension Activity: Literary Analysis

MONSTER MASH
A LITERARY ANALYSIS TASK

In this unit, we have explored the idea of monsters:

- How do we define the term "monster?"
- Are monsters born or created?
- Can monsters be redeemed?

Now, you will have a chance to explore how your text treats the idea of monsters. Select two foil characters from your story (at least one of whom should be understood to be somewhat "monstrous") and explore how they are characterized in your book. Then, using only direct quotes from your text, create a "Monster Mash" where you mashup key details from the story to explore how these characters work together to reveal an understanding of what it means to be a monster.

Your submission should include a written rationale in which you explain your choices.

Artfulness

Figure 4.11

LITERARY PLAYLIST

Congratulations, Writers! Over the course of this marking period, you have learned a variety of skills that will help you shape and control your writing to deliver your desired message. Now, it's time to celebrate your learning!

You and your Writing Team will work together to develop a literary playlist featuring a variety of original creations (prose creations; not actual music) that work together to develop a shared message. Like any good playlist, your Team creation will feature a selection of individual pieces (a minimum of one per Writer) that stand on their own as individual texts but which are designed to work together to deliver a unified message on a topic of your choosing. In addition, the sequence in which your pieces are "played" should be determined by how each piece functions to develop a logical line of reasoning.

The Group Task:

As a Team, identify one "true story" issue or event that will serve as the unifying element of your playlist. Then, consider what message you would like your overall playlist to reveal about this issue or event and how you would like to move your reader through your argument. Your Team may wish to consider:

- Is your unifying idea fairly straightforward or is it complicated by alternative/multiple perspectives?
  - o If the former, what element of your topic would you like your playlist to focus on and develop?
  - o If the latter, do you want to take a side on the issue or event, or do you want your reader to experience the tension between opposing ideas?
- Do you want your playlist to explore concrete or abstract ideas associated with your issue or event?
- What emotions do you seek to tap into with your playlist? What musical genres best reflect those emotions?
- What overall message do you want to convey to your reader and how should you sequence your playlist to achieve the desired effect?

Based on your responses to the questions above, as well as any other questions you feel may be useful in developing this project, brainstorm how best to achieve your vision. The individual pieces should be designed to harmonize with one another to develop a cohesive exploration of your topic.

The Individual Task:

One of the requirements of this task is that your creative writing reflects the musicality we have explored this quarter. Therefore, each narrative should be written in a way that meaningfully reflects an inspirational song.

Figure 4.11 continued

To complete this task, determine if you would like to work with an existing Writer's Notebook draft or if you would prefer to create an entirely new narrative. Then, identify a song that you feel captures the essence of what you are hoping to convey (based upon tone, mood, lyrics, or some other criteria) and use that song to inspire your original fictional narrative.

Assessment Requirements:

Group Presentation: Each Team will present highlights of the complete playlist to the larger class, exploring the central theme of the playlist, the individual texts included on the list with a brief summary of what each text explores, and an explanation of the choices made as a group, including how the Team decided to structure and organize the playlist.

Individual Submission: Each Team member will submit their individual creation and self-reflection for an assessment score. As part of the reflection, be sure to address:

➤ How the brainstorming stage of the activity informed the selection of your own unique narrative including how your individual piece connected to and supported the shared vision of the larger Writing Team

➤ What message you hoped to convey with your individual piece (your writing objective)

➤ What song served as your inspiration and why, and

➤ How and where you attempted to adjust your narrative to reflect your inspiration song.

5
Chapter

Look Inside Chapter 5

SCAN ME

Scan to access
supplemental
resources

 *Artfulness*

Windows
Prep Time: High

Description:

In this lesson, students experiment with writing as a window into the world by considering the inspiration one gleaned from looking closely at one small portion of their lives. To conduct this activity, students are provided with a detailed image and a small picture frame. They move the picture frame over the image to capture one small piece of the moment. Then, they write the story captured in their "window" into that world.

 When selecting images, determine if you would like to focus on characterization, setting, selection of details, contrasts, or a variety of the above and then source photos that match your learning objectives.

To save money on the frames, consider making them out of printer paper. Use the QR code at the front of this Chapter to see step-by-step instructions.

Student-Friendly Objectives:

By the end of this lesson, students will be able to:

- Elaborate on specific details by exploring a small portion of a world rather than trying to capture the entire environment from which they seek inspiration

- Understand writing as a tool for artistic expression rather than one solely concerned with communicating universal messages

Materials:

- A variety of images of famous "unconventional" art posted around the room (for example, Andy Warhol's, *Campbell's Soup Cans* or Salvador Dali's, *The Persistence of Memory*)

- Excerpt from the Preface of Henry James', *The Portrait of a Lady*

- Class copies of images rich in detail, printed on standard 8.5" x 11" paper

- Very small picture frames or photo mats (5 x 7 or smaller)

Rationale:

Many authors have argued that their writing is not intended to "send a message" but to expose a unique aspect of life. In essence, they argue, their writing presents a window into life.

With so much emphasis on thematic exploration, however, the idea of writing as art—as something intended simply to capture the essence of an idea—can sometimes get lost. This activity forces students to recognize the artistic value of writing and how it can be used as a tool for exploration and expression rather than as a tool to "send a message" to the reader. This is a particularly useful activity to complete when paired with difficult readings or readings in which the characters are uniquely grotesque.

Through this activity, students learn that art is about seeing beyond the surface, exploring the nooks and crannies of life that are hidden, sometimes, in plain sight. They come to value all expression as artistic expression and, as such, discover their ability to explore topics of their choosing without fear or concern that they are "seeing" something incorrectly or are expressing something that is too unconventional. By demonstrating to them that writing can simply be an expression of an idea rather than a "lesson" or a "message" to be conveyed, students come to see writing as a form of art and, in the process, gain a clearer understanding of why our courses are called "Language *Arts*" classes rather than "English" classes.

Anticipatory Activity (20 minutes):
Before students enter the room, post images of famous unconventional art around the room.

Once students are settled at their desks, ask them to select any one image from around the room and spend five minutes writing a response to that image in their Writer's Notebook. After five minutes, ask for two or three volunteers to share their responses, making sure that students continue the practice of reading exactly what they have written as opposed to summarizing their thoughts. Then, extend the discussion by asking if any students are familiar with the images and/or what their thoughts are regarding whether these images constitute "art."

Next, share the excerpt from the Preface to Henry James', *The Portrait of a Lady* with students (provided in **Figure 5.1**) and briefly discuss his argument to check for understanding.

Return to discussing the art around the room. With their new understanding of art as a window into the world, ask students to spend five minutes writing an updated response to their originally selected image; then ask a few students to share how their response to the art changed when they explored it as an expression of an idea or a window into life. Conclude by asking: What is the connection between visual art, such as the art around the room, and written art such as novels, and how can keeping the artistic element in mind help us more thoughtfully consider an author's writing?

Figure 5.1 from page 143

Henry James Excerpt

The house of fiction has in short not one window, but a million—a number of possible windows not to be reckoned, rather; every one of which has been pierced, or is still pierceable, in its vast front, by the need of the individual vision and by the pressure of the individual will. These apertures, of dissimilar shape and size, hang so, all together, over the human scene that we might have expected of them a greater sameness of report than we find. They are but windows at the best, mere holes in a dead wall, disconnected, perched aloft; they are not hinged doors opening straight upon life. But they have this mark of their own that at each of them stands a figure with a pair of eyes, or at least with a field-glass, which forms, again and again, for observation, a unique instrument, insuring to the person making use of it an impression distinct from every other. He and his neighbours are watching the same show, but one seeing more where the other sees less, one seeing black where the other sees white, one seeing big where the other sees small, one seeing coarse where the other sees fine. And so on, and so on…

James, H. (n.d.). *Preface to The Portrait of a Lady*. The Literature Network. http://www.online-literature.com/henry_james/portrait_lady/0/.

Process (5 minutes):
Provide students with copies of the photo images you sourced in advance of this activity. These images should not be posted around the room; rather each student should be able to place their image on their desks. Also provide each student with their own mini frame.

Instruct students to slide their frame over the image until they capture the window (the frame of details from the image) they want to explore in writing. **Figure 5.2** provides some suggested approaches to this portion of the activity and the potential effect of each approach on student learning.

Drafting (30 minutes):
Students will now draft for thirty minutes, creating a detailed vignette of their window while being careful to emphasize whatever literary element(s) the teacher has connected to this activity (e.g., characterization, setting, selection of details, etc.). Stress to students that rather than writing a full story during this time, they should focus on elaboration by expanding upon the details they see in their inspiration window to fill their writing time.

> **Figure 5.2**
>
> ## Approach Options
>
> - Asking students to select their own image and their own window will maximize the cultural responsiveness of this activity by giving considerable agency and voice to each student.
>
> - Asking Writing Teams to select the same image but choose their own window independent of the Team will showcase the effect of authorial choice on understanding by revealing, in particular, how the selection of detail shapes a text.
>
> - Asking partners within each Writing Team to work from both the same image and the same window will emphasize James' argument that although students and their "Neighbours are watching the same show . . . one [is] seeing more where the other sees less . . . And so on, and so on . . ."

Writing Team Share (25 minutes):
Have students share their stories with their Writing Team. Depending on the window approach you selected in the process stage above, after each share, ask the Writing Team to either identify the window the student was working with or compare and contrast how students looking through the same window arrived at a different story. Each member of the Writing Team should share their stories before moving on to the Reflection stage.

Reflection (10 minutes):
As a closing activity, ask students to reflect in their Writer's Notebook about the process for today's activity.

- How did viewing their writing as a window to a world affect the approach they took to their writing?

- In what ways did treating writing as a form of artistic expression liberate their writing options?

- In what ways did treating writing as a form of artistic expression restrict their writing options?

- How might they be able to purposefully incorporate this approach into a variety of writing tasks in the future?

Differentiate

To Support:

To support younger/struggling learners, include an observation activity that will help them capture their observations based upon the window they select. One strategy that I have found works with most learners is to ask students to visualize the image divided into quadrants and then make a list of every observation they make for each quadrant. This will allow students to focus closely on smaller chunks of their window and will help them notice minute details that may otherwise escape their attention.

To Challenge:

To challenge advanced learners, ask them to conduct this activity twice—once to tell the broader story of the full image and once to capture a narrower window. This will help them focus their end-of-activity reflection on the comparative aspect of expansive vs. narrow writing and will give them a new perspective on what it means to either expand upon a moment or home in on small details. If you elect this challenge activity, you may want to spread this lesson out over two days to ensure students have sufficient time to complete the drafting. I would also recommend waiting until you begin the window activity before you explore *The Portrait of a Lady* preface excerpt to avoid affecting students' work on the full image activity on Day 1.

Suggested Unit Integration:

Consider integrating this lesson into a beginning-of-year instructional unit by asking students to ponder the Essential Question: What is the role of fiction in our everyday lives? Then, provide paired readings that complement this lesson such as Virginia Woolf's short story, *An Unwritten Novel,* Ken Liu's short story, *The Paper Menagerie,* Li-Young Lee's poem, "A Story," or Salman Rushdie's novel, *Haroun and the Sea of Stories.*

Later in the school year, this lesson would pair well with book units that raise difficult issues and/or that have complex (perhaps even unlikeable) protagonists. It would also work well with character-driven stories that have ambiguous endings which may leave the reader wondering *So what?* such as Shirley Jackson's, *We Have Always Lived in the Castle.*

By focusing on writing as a form of artistic expression, students will recognize that, despite our frequent emphasis on thematic explorations, fictional writing can be as much about exploring an idea as it is about revealing a message.

146

Extension Activity:

- *Personal Narrative:* Ask students to photograph their environment every day for one or two weeks. Their photos should feature small, seemingly random everyday elements of their lives. Once they have compiled a collection of images, they should select four to five images to turn into a collection of connected vignettes whose sole purpose is to serve as a window into their everyday lives.

- *Research:* Ask students to research one of the authors studied in your whole-class readings. Then, ask them to either write an essay or develop a presentation that explores how the author's own biographical information leads to an understanding of what window into life they may have been exploring when they created the text read in class, being sure that students provide evidence both from their research sources as well as the whole-class text.

- *Visual Media:* Follow the instructions for the "Personal Narrative" activity above except require that students present their work as a photo essay, collage, or another form of visual media. Each vignette should be paired with a corresponding visual, either the actual photo they captured or an original interpretation of that photo. This variation would be a great way to differentiate your instruction for students who are visual and/or artistic learners (see **Figure 5.3** for sample instructions for this extension activity).

Figure 5.3

Extension Activity: Visual Media

Spring is a time of transformation. As we emerge from the cold embrace of winter, we are welcomed into a world of new possibilities. During our Writing Wednesday lesson, *Windows*, we explored how the written word can take the form of art, pausing to explore an aspect of our lives without necessarily concerning itself with a larger message. Now it's your turn to explore your world through written art, exploring and capturing the essence of transformation in your own original writing.

Directions: Over the next four weeks, identify one natural element of your environment that will be changing as spring emerges. Take pictures of your chosen element at different times, capturing the transformation it experiences with the passage of time. Consider if you want to capture that element at different times of the day or at the same time of day over a span of several weeks.

Figure 5.3 continued

Once you have compiled a collection of images, select five (5) images to develop into an artistic creation that features a blend of visual and written text.

For each image you select, determine if you want to showcase the exact image or an original interpretation of that image. Interpretations may include, for example:

- The image of the photo with a filter applied
- A hand-drawn sketch
- Digital art
- Pop art
- Cartoon
- Mosaic
- Film

Then, for each image, develop an accompanying narrative in the genre of your choosing. For example:

- Short story
- Vignette
- Music lyrics
- Slam poetry
- Journal entry
- Graphic novel

You have creative license regarding the format of your final product. You may elect to develop one cohesive narrative that is inspired by each of your five images, or you may elect to develop a collection of individual short texts that work together to form a cohesive picture of your world.

As always, consider the purpose and effect of your choices. What window are you seeking to explore and how will your visual and written elements work together to create the image revealed through that window? You will present your work to your classmates as part of your assessment.

Reflection:

As part of your submission project, be sure to include a written reflection that:

➤ Explores how your natural element transformed over the course of your monitoring and what elements of that transformation you were seeking to capture

➤ Explains the connection between each of the images and their accompanying text, using specific details from the visual and written elements for support

➤ Explores how and why you selected your writing format, and

➤ Discusses how you assembled/organized your work and how that choice supported your writing objective.

So Stylish
Prep Time: Medium

Description:
Gaining inspiration from music, students will listen to two different versions of the same song in order to appreciate how tempo, rhythm, and other creative devices affect tone and mood. Once students have completed the music-based anticipatory activity, they will experiment with adjusting and controlling the style of a sample written text before revising one of their own drafts to better control stylistic elements such as structure, punctuation, syntax, and diction.

Student-Friendly Objectives:	*Materials:*
By the end of this lesson, students will be able to: • Recognize how stylistic choices such as syntax, diction, and punctuation shape the written word • Make informed decisions about stylistic choices in order to support and advance their writing goals	• Audio versions of paired songs • Sample excerpt from a text for students to revise

Rationale:
Style is such an important component of developing an authentic Writer's Voice and yet the idea that writing is a series of choices that should include consideration not only of content but also of style is often lost in the rush to meet the seemingly more important educational standards. By showcasing a variety of ways to express the same idea and demonstrating to students how stylistic choices can affect the way a reader understands a work, we highlight the value of making thoughtful, deliberate stylistic choices. Students come to understand that considering the reader's experience has value and that controlling the reader's experience by adjusting the style and pacing of their writing can advance and support their writing goals.

Anticipatory Activity (10 minutes):
Play two versions of a selected song, ideally one where there are significant differences between the two versions. Some sample pairings

are provided in **Figure 5.4**. As always, make sure you are using your selected works with appropriate permission.

Figure 5.4

Examples of Paired Songs to Explore With Students

"Red Red Wine" • Neil Diamond • UB40	"I Will Always Love You" • Dolly Parton • Whitney Houston
"Sleep to Dream" • Fiona Apple • Bettye LaVette	"Personal Jesus" • Depeche Mode • Johnny Cash
"Tainted Love" • Gloria Jones • Soft Cell	"Big Yellow Taxi" • Joni Mitchell • Counting Crows

---

As students listen, ask them to compare and contrast each version of the song in the Observation section of their Writer's Notebook, focusing on how the differences between each version shape the listeners' experience and understanding of the song.

Once students have made their observations, ask for a few volunteers to share their findings and then discuss as a class how stylistic choices such as tempo and rhythm affect the tone and mood of the songs.

Process (25 minutes):
Provide Writing Teams with a small excerpt from a reading of your choice. Ideally, this excerpt will be somewhat dense with little or no dialogue. Before making your class copies, be sure to remove all punctuation, line, and paragraphs breaks from the passage so that the students receive only the raw text (words only).

In their Writing Teams, students should work together to revise the provided passage two different times by adding punctuation as well as line, and/or paragraph breaks where desired. Their goal is to ensure that each version creates a noticeably different experience—and ideally a noticeably different understanding—of the passage. Although you can ask Teams to use a different color of ink to differentiate the two versions, this activity works best by providing Teams with two copies of the same passage so they can more easily compare their revisions.

At the end of the activity, ask for volunteers to share what they observed as they moved through this process and how this activity affected their understanding of style. Then, ask Writing Teams to post their two versions around the room for a gallery walk experience to serve as inspiration during the drafting stage. As an alternative to a gallery walk, if students have their own technology in class, ask them to post their variations to a shared online discussion board for other Writing Teams to explore and review.

 Be careful with pacing during this step. It's easy for Teams to get bogged down with their punctuation and style decisions (although the grammar discussions this activity encourages makes the lost time worthwhile), so providing a relatively short passage or breaking this lesson into two days to provide more time in the early stages may be a good option, particularly with younger students.

Drafting (40 minutes):

Individually, students will now select one of their previous writing drafts to revise for style with an emphasis on revising the pacing of their work. Once they have selected the draft to revise, students should consider what effect they are trying to achieve.

- Is there a particular tone or mood that would work well for their piece?

- Are there places where they want the reader to move slower or faster? If so, where and why?

- How will they use a combination of syntax, diction, punctuation, and visual breaks (such as line/paragraph breaks) to achieve their goals?

Writing Team Share (10 minutes):
Students will share excerpts from their original and revised pieces with their Writing Teams, being careful to explain what effect they were hoping to achieve with their revisions and what strategies they employed to achieve that effect.

Artfulness

Reflection: (5 minutes):
In the final five minutes of class, students should reflect in their Writer's Notebook about this activity.

- What effect were they hoping to achieve with their revision and what strategies did they employ in an effort to support their writing goal?

- Do they feel they were successful? Why or why not?

- How can they use the knowledge gained in this activity when crafting their own writing pieces in the future?

Differentiate

As you decide when to incorporate this activity, remember that students will need to select from one of their own drafts in their Writer's Notebook to revise so it may be best to wait until you are far enough into the school year that they have a reasonable number of drafts to select from. If you would like to use this lesson earlier in the year, consider having them select from one of their formal written assignments they previously submitted to you for a grade as their revision piece.

To Support:
To support younger/struggling learners, it may be a good idea to break this lesson into two days—one to explore and practice with the writing of others, and one to revise their own work. Support their learning further by providing a set of notes with examples of different types of syntax structures, sample printed passages that have been rewritten in a variety of ways to adjust pacing, and perhaps a brief set of notes explaining how diction—and particularly, the syllable count of different words—can also function to control reading pace.

To Challenge:
Challenge advanced learners by providing a specific mood or tone you want them to target as they revise or turn this activity into a Writing Team challenge where other Teams can either select the piece to be revised or determine what tone/mood students must work towards during their revision process.

Alternatively, require students to rewrite their selected draft more than once to demonstrate their control of style.

Suggested Unit Integration:
This lesson pairs well both with shorter pieces such as poetry and longer narrative fiction. If you are completing this lesson earlier in the year, consider pairing it with a poetry exploration to show students how poets use literary elements such as syntax, diction, and punctuation to create rhythm. If you are completing this lesson later in the year, consider pairing it with any whole-class reading you are currently conducting or revisit work you have explored earlier in the year with a new focus.

Extension Activity:

- *Creative Writing and Revision:* Ask students to revise an original draft into a Publication Piece, making deliberate stylistic choices that shape the reader's experience of the text. Then, have them swap their writing with another student to produce a "cover" version of each text which develops an entirely new experience for the reader (see **Figure 5.5** for sample instructions for this extension activity).

- *Literary Analysis:* Ask students to review poems or short stories that develop a strong sense of rhythm or style such as those written by Emily Dickinson, Gwendolyn Brooks, or Virginia Woolf and then write a literary analysis essay that argues how the author uses stylistic elements to affect meaning.

- *Multimedia Research Presentation:* Ask students to create a multimedia presentation that explores a songwriter who created a cover version of an earlier song. What changes did that songwriter make and why? How does the tempo and rhythm of each version affect the listener's understanding of the song?

Figure 5.5

Extension Activity: Cover Me!

Individually: Develop one of your original narratives into a full-length Publication Piece. During the revision process, carefully consider the effect you are trying to achieve with your piece and make deliberate stylistic choices that support your goals.

Thoughtfully employ no fewer than three of the following stylistic techniques to control your reader's pacing:

- Diction
- Syntax
- Asyndeton
- Polysyndeton
- Dialogue
- Punctuation
- Line Breaks
- Paragraph Breaks

With a Partner: Once you have your Publication Piece completed, swap your text with a partner of your choice. When you receive your partner's work, rewrite that piece as a "cover piece" in order to create a completely new effect for the reader.

"Cover" Requirements:

- Keep the original wording (and sequence) largely the same, only adding or replacing words as absolutely necessary to clarify meaning.

- Incorporating no fewer than three of the stylistic techniques identified above, revise the tempo, rhythm, and/or tone of your partner's piece to achieve your desired effect which should differ from the effect the original piece created.

As part of your submission, you should include a written rationale that explains your choices <u>for both your original Publication Piece and your "cover" piece</u>. Your rationale should explain which stylistic techniques you employed in each piece and how they were intended to achieve your desired effect.

Story Steal—Crime & Punishment
Prep Time: Low

Description:
In this activity, Writing Teams are paired up against one another to "steal" the story of an opposing Team member. The drafting begins simply enough—students are given a writing prompt and they begin creating their narrative. At a pre-determined time during the activity, however, Team members are told to swap their stories with a member of an opposing Team. The opposing Team member reads their partner's story and highlights sentences they want to "steal" from the author. Any sentence that is highlighted must be removed from the draft and the author will have to reevaluate how to continue the story with those lines removed. There is another catch, however. Later in the activity, the students who "stole" the lines will be required to incorporate a select number of those sentences, exactly as written, into their own original narrative!

Student-Friendly Objectives:	*Materials:*
By the end of this lesson, students will be able to:	
• Plan and organize ideas for writing	• Story prompts
• Reimagine and revise writing to address a variety of purposes	• Highlighters (one per student)

Rationale:
I love low-prep, highly effective creative writing tasks, and this activity checks both of those boxes. Capable of being thrown together at a moment's notice, this lesson challenges students' creative writing skills, promotes critical thinking, and requires thoughtful revision. Although it has the feel of a game, the challenge level here is pretty high. First, students must plan and organize their writing to fit the assigned writing prompt. When they conduct the "crime," (the initial steal) they must critically evaluate their partner's work to determine which components of the story to omit—either because of their relative strengths or weaknesses. After their lines have been stolen, students must consider how best to revise their story to account for the pilfered components.

The "punishment" challenge forces students to take their writing through another round of revision, this time while celebrating the work of the other student. By the time this activity concludes, students will have used critical thinking skills to take their writing through a nearly complete writing process cycle.

Figure 5.6

The Crime: Students steal four to six sentences from their partner's work, preventing their partner from using those sentences in their stories.

The Punishment:
The "thief" has to incorporate at least two of the stolen sentences—selected by the victim—to incorporate, verbatim, into their own narrative.

Drafting (25 minutes):
Arrange students in two sets of Writing Teams so that members of an opposing Writing Team are seated across from one another. Provide a writing prompt to your students. Determine whether you want all students writing to the same prompt or whether each student will work from a unique prompt. Then, allow students twenty-five minutes of uninterrupted drafting time.

The Crime—Story Steal (10 minutes):
After students have been drafting for twenty-five minutes, ask them to complete the sentence they are working on and put their pencils down. Then have them swap their narratives with the member of the

156

opposing Team sitting across from them. Students will now read their partner's story with a highlighter in their hand. Instruct students to highlight a minimum of four and a maximum of six sentences with the understanding that whatever they highlight will be considered "stolen" from their partner. Once a sentence has been stolen, their partner can no longer use it in their narrative. After the stolen sentences have been identified and highlighted, partners return the story to its original author for revision.

Revision (20 minutes):
Students must now revise their story to allow for a cohesive, unified narrative that does not include the stolen sentences. They are welcome to completely rewrite those sentences into something new, add in additional lines to address the necessary transitions, or simply omit them and keep going, but the story must flow in a logical and effective manner without the stolen sentences. Students will spend twenty minutes revising to recover from the theft of their work.

The Punishment—Payback: (15 minutes):
At this point, students will be required to incorporate, verbatim, at least two of the sentences they've stolen from their partner into their own writing, and they must do so in an effective and unified manner. But there's a catch. The student who had their work stolen is the one who gets to decide which lines the thief has to use in their narrative! Once their "punishment" has been handed down, students will have the remainder of this time to revise their drafts to incorporate these new lines. They can incorporate these sentences anywhere in their narrative, even by adding them into portions they have previously drafted.

Writing Team Share (20 minutes):
Writing Teams will spend the final twenty minutes of class reading the narratives they developed with one another. To manage pacing concerns, I recommend splitting students up into groups of four with two members of each Writing Team (ideally, partnered members) serving as one group for the end-of-class share.

Differentiate

To Support:	*To Challenge:*
Support younger/struggling learners by carefully considering who to partner them up with to avoid hurt feelings or an overly competitive pairing. If you know students are shy or suffer from anxiety, for example, plan in advance who you think might allow them to enjoy this activity in a supportive and friendly manner. You may also want to consider reducing the number of stolen lines to make this challenge a bit more manageable for emerging Writers.	The easiest way to increase the rigor with this activity is to increase the number of stolen lines or to throw in additional "required" elements during the drafting time above and beyond the crime and punishment elements. The more twists you incorporate, the harder the challenge will be.

Suggested Unit Integration:

This activity pairs beautifully with any instruction on the writing process. Rather than delivering a lecture on the writing process with the various steps of the process outlined in a linear format, have students complete this lesson in anticipation of the larger writing unit. Once students have spent the day completing this *Story Steal* activity, they will be primed to understand the brainstorming, drafting, editing, and revision process in a way that is concrete, and therefore, meaningful to them. They will likely have realized during this process that revision can be sloppy—sentences get added and rearranged seemingly on a whim, we try things out that don't work and have to try again, etc. In this manner, students will come to understand, through experiential learning, that while we often list the steps of the writing process in sequence for ease of organization, the reality of the writing process is a bit more chaotic—and that's okay!

Extension Activity:

- *Literary Comparative Analysis:* Provide students with draft and final versions of published texts which showcase side-by-side passages of the same moment or scene. Then, ask students to conduct a comparative analysis exploring the differences between both versions and the effect the revisions have on the reader's understanding of the text.

- *Writing Process—Technology Strands:* Deepen students' understanding of the Writing Process while simultaneously expanding their understanding of the word processing tools available to them by having them take any draft through the writing process while using Track Changes or a similar word processing tool. Rather than a polished piece of writing, their submission will be the Track Changes (or similar) version of their work that shows all the edits and revisions they made as they worked. They will conclude their submission with a reflection that evaluates how the writing process helped them grow as a Writer and the role the accompanying technology tool(s) played in helping them develop and hone their craft (see **Figure 5.7** for sample instructions for this extension activity).

- *Vocabulary:* Have students update their Technical Vocabulary list to include or revise their entry for "writing process" (and any accompanying steps you choose to highlight) in a manner that reflects what they have learned about the writing process and its steps as a result of this activity.

Figure 5.7

Extension Activity: Scratch That!

You have learned that, in real life, the writing process is not a set of neat, linear steps that Writers complete to bring a text to publication, but rather a messy process that involves trial, error, and a whole lot of scratched out text. Now, you will demonstrate what you know of the writing process as you utilize modern tools of the trade to assist with your revisions.

Directions: For this activity, you will be submitting a Track Changes version of your Publication Piece that showcases the revisions you made while bringing your piece to its final version.

Step 1: Select a draft from your Writer's Notebook that you would like to revise as a Publication Piece. Then, type that draft—verbatim—into a Word document.

Step 2: Turn on Track Changes to show all the revisions and edits you make as you work. Take your draft through the writing process until you are satisfied with the final product.

Step 3: Submit your work with the Track Changes still visible. (Do NOT submit a clean copy of your Publication Piece.)

As part of your submission, you should include a written reflection that

➤ Provides an overview of the changes you made while you worked and why you made those changes

➤ Evaluates how the writing process helped you achieve your goals for this piece, being sure to cite specific examples from your work to support your claims, and

➤ Explores how word processing tools such Track Changes helped you to recognize the work that goes into the writing process.

159

Writing Makeover
Prep Time: Low

Description:

This is an individual activity that asks students to revisit their previous drafts and then select one draft to reimagine as a modern, technology-based storytelling genre such as a podcast, a photo post, a graphic novel, or the like. Although each student will be reimagining one of their own pieces for the makeover, they will work with their Writing Teams during the selection and brainstorming stages to ensure each Team member has the support they need to develop an effective makeover for their writing.

Student-Friendly Objectives:	*Materials:*
By the end of this lesson, students will be able to:	
<ul><li>Thoughtfully evaluate their writing and the writing of others</li><li>Understand the impact of genre on meaning</li></ul>	<ul><li>All students will need access to prior drafts of their work</li></ul>

Rationale:

Too often in our classrooms, we assign writing that is designed exclusively for publication. By this, I mean that we only ask students to write work that we know we will be grading. While this is perfectly understandable as a sanity-saver for teachers, for our students, it creates the impression that writing is a chore that is only completed when absolutely necessary and only to achieve a very narrow set of objectives. In addition, it puts pressure on students to be perfect rather than thoughtful. It produces students who write to earn the "A" rather than writers who are willing to take risks in order to improve.

By treating the drafts produced in their Writer's Notebooks as inspiration rather than finished products, students come to recognize that all writing has value. Even an "imperfect" product that was written in a timed environment for a narrow purpose can be reimagined as something new and exciting. In fact, this lesson emphasizes that sometimes the very imperfections in our writing are what gives it value—it becomes recognized for its *potential* rather than its face value.

Allowing each Team member to select and share one of their drafts with the goal of reimagining it gives each Writer a voice and value in their Team. Having Team members focus on the potential, rather than the shortcomings, in each draft further emphasizes writing as a process to be refined rather than a one-time event.

Anticipatory Activity (10 minutes):
Ask individual students to review their previous Writer's Notebook drafts and identify two or three pieces that they believe have the potential to be reimagined as a new genre with an emphasis on modern storytelling techniques such as blogs, performance videos, video games, and podcasts. Students should understand that they will be asked to both present their original drafts to their Writing Team as well as provide their explanation for what genre(s) they think may work well with each draft and why.

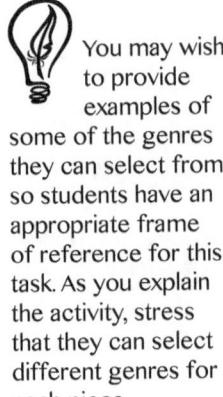 You may wish to provide examples of some of the genres they can select from so students have an appropriate frame of reference for this task. As you explain the activity, stress that they can select different genres for each piece.

Text Selection (30 minutes):
Writing Teams will spend thirty minutes sharing their revision candidates, proposed new genres, and rationales. Then, the Team members will evaluate the merits of each student's proposal and help each student select the best draft/genre to target for a "makeover." Depending on the size of each Writing Team and/or the number of revision candidates each student puts forward, you may want to suggest that Teams break down into pairs to allow more time for each student to share and receive thoughtful feedback.

Brainstorming/Outlining (40 minutes):
Once each Team member has received quality feedback and revision suggestions, they will spend all but the last ten minutes of class time outlining their proposed revision. They will likely only have time to create a detailed brainstorm of the changes they would like to see. For example, if they envision their draft as a video game narrative, they will likely be able to outline, but not create, each level of the game. However, they should set a goal to have a complete outline by the end of their work time.

Reflection (10 minutes):
Students should spend the final ten minutes of this activity reflecting on the process of reimagining their drafts in a new light.

- How did they evaluate each of their drafts before selecting the candidates to present to their Team members?

- How was the Team able to help them select the best piece and brainstorm the genre conversion?

- What did they need to adjust in order to fit their piece into the new genre?

- What unexpected improvements or struggles did they encounter when they began outlining their work?

- How do they feel about the draft in this new genre relative to the original draft?

- What have they learned about genre as a result of this process?

Differentiate

To Support:
Younger/struggling learners may need a variety of supports to be successful with today's lesson. One of the easiest supports we can offer is more time. Consider extending this activity over two or more days to allow students to properly reflect upon and brainstorm their work—they are not likely to feel successful if they are stressed about pacing.

Supports can also be offered by conferencing with students one-on-one before or during their work time. Presenting this as a partner activity where Team members pair up to select one draft per pair to collaborate on together could also be effective.

Finally, graphic organizers are a great way to support learners who need concrete guidance on what steps to take. Be sure to keep the graphic organizer broad enough so that students have to do the critical thinking portion themselves, but narrow enough to give them clear process steps to follow as a guide.

To Challenge:
Ask students to reimagine the same draft in two different genres, complete a detailed outline for each version of the draft, and then select the one they feel is the most successful, being sure to explain their rationale for that choice. Extend the challenge by asking them to write a detailed compare/contrast analysis of each version and use that comparison to write a formal evaluation *of their own work* as if they were conducting a standard literary analysis of a published text.

Suggested Unit Integration:
This is a great activity to pair with comparative analysis. Incorporate comparative analysis into your instructional units by comparing and

contrasting excerpts from historical fiction to nonfiction memoirs, or poetry to prose passages to evaluate how the genre shapes both the author's craft and the reader's understanding of the text. Then, use this lesson to extend students' understanding of the comparative framework by exploring how comparative analysis functions not only as an external evaluation tool, but as an internal evaluation tool when creating their own products.

Extension Activity:

- *Literary/Nonfiction Analysis:* Provide students with an excerpt from a published text (or have them source their own passage). Then, ask students to rewrite this passage in a new genre, focusing on modernization. In other words, rather than asking them to convert a poem to a prose passage, or a vignette into a short story, ask students to convert the passage into a graphic novel, a podcast, a blog, or a listicle. As part of the assignment, ask students to provide a detailed rationale explaining their choices and evaluating the effect of each genre on both authorial choice and the reader's understanding (see **Figure 5.8** for sample instructions for this extension activity).

Figure 5.8

Extension Activity: A Fresh Face

Directions: Put a new spin on your class text. Select any passage between two and six pages in length and reimagine this passage in a modern genre. Your goal is to maintain the same overall feel and intention of the passage, while aligning it with emerging writing genres. Select from any one of the following genres or propose a genre of your own choosing (subject to teacher approval):

- Podcast
- Tik Tok Video
- Listicle

- Blog
- Graphic Novel
- Instagram Post

Submission Requirements:

- ☐ A copy of the original passage that served as your inspiration for the update
- ☐ Your reimagined draft in its new genre, and
- ☐ A written rationale that explains your choices and evaluates the effect of your chosen genre on both the content and style choices you made and the reader's understanding.

- *Persuasion:* Ask students to create an elevator pitch and/or a formal proposal that seeks approval on the genre conversion. Using the work they conducted today, they will need to highlight why reimagining the original narrative in this new genre is an effective strategy, using evidence from both the original narrative and the outline to support their claim.

- *Research:* Ask students to research modern communication genres such as podcasts, graphic novels, blogs, and vlogs. They should explore the origins of this communication genre and the industries with which it is most commonly associated. As part of their research, they should explore the key conventions of this genre as well as its advantages and disadvantages. Finally, they should present their findings to the class as part of a formal multimedia presentation which incorporates elements of their assigned genre.

Story Saboteur
Prep Time: High

Description:

This lesson was inspired by my favorite former Food Network Television show, *Cutthroat Kitchen*. In this lesson, students are given a genre of writing in which to draft and a story prompt that leads them in a particular direction. However, as the drafting stage continues, members from opposing Writing Teams can purchase sabotage items that force the other Writers to incorporate (or exclude) specific story elements, potentially resulting in an ineffective final narrative. The winning Writer for each game is determined by adding up the rubric score earned on their final narrative and the number of purchase tokens they have remaining at the end of the game.

Student-Friendly Objectives: By the end of this lesson, students will be able to:	*Materials:*
• Generate, plan, and organize ideas for writing • Consider alternative approaches to narrative construction • Revise content and style to address a specific genre and goal	• Purchase tokens such as toy money, poker chips, color-coded slips of paper • Story genres and prompts • List of sabotage items for purchase (3/game)

Rationale:

Although developing effective sabotage elements may take a bit of preparation on the part of the teacher, this activity is well worth the investment! Students love competition and this activity challenges them to compete in a manner that first requires them to evaluate, acknowledge, and respect their competitors before they can effectively sabotage them in the name of the "win."

In addition, this game incorporates a review of genre and literary elements, requires reflection and critical thinking, and engages students in the writing process with an emphasis on revision. Finally, the game promotes collaboration as winning Teams are determined, not by the strengths of individual Writing Team members, but by their cumulative efforts to succeed.

Artfulness

The Set Up (10 minutes):

Arrange students into competitive teams of between three and four students each and provide each student a predetermined amount of purchase tokens. There should be no more than one member of any original Writing Team per competitive team. If you have an odd number of students, ask the larger Teams to select one Team member to serve as a host, rather than a player, for one of the competitions. Then, as a class, go over the rules which are found in **Figure 5.9**.

While the set up can occur in ten minutes with proper planning, failure to plan may slow you down considerably. I strongly recommend that in the day or two leading up to this lesson, you plan how to administer this game in each of your instructional blocks. Different blocks of students may have an odd number of students or different student populations who require differentiated approaches, so ensuring you are prepared for a variety of contingencies before game day will allow you to move through the set up stage efficiently, maximizing game time.

Figure 5.9

Rules of the Game

Each competitive Writer is trying to win their "heat" and the winner is determined by adding together the rubric score on their final story and the number of purchase tokens left over at the end of the game. The student with the highest combined score wins that heat, but the winning Team will be determined by adding up all of the corresponding Team member scores across all heats—the Team with the highest cumulative score wins the entire game day challenge.

During the course of the game, three sabotages will be introduced. Each Writer has the option to purchase any or all of the sabotage items. Sabotage items are purchased in auction format: the highest bidder wins the sabotage. Student bids cannot exceed the number of purchase tokens they have remaining at the time of the auction.

Round 1 (15 minutes):

Assign each competitive team their genre and writing prompt (this can be identical for all competitive teams or can be differentiated as desired). For example:

- Genre: Dystopian

- Setting: The year is 3415 and the characters are located in South Asia

- Conflict: Global water shortages lead to a resource scramble—powerful government controls who has access to resources

Once competitive teams have their story prompt, provide two minutes for them to brainstorm a story recipe (see **Figure 2.8** in Chapter 2 for a Story Recipe template). Then, interrupt them for the first auction.

Quickly describe the first auction component. You can find some sample story sabotages to use during the auctions in **Figure 5.10**. You can also source sabotage elements by reviewing the "challenge" sections of earlier *Artfulness* lessons or by incorporating techniques found in the whole-class texts you've worked with throughout the year. The key is to make each auction item something that either significantly increases the challenge level or simply doesn't fit with the original story prompt. When developing the sabotage elements to auction, use your imagination and have fun!

Hold the auction and sell the sabotage to the highest bidder. Depending on the terms of the purchase, the buyer can either assign the sabotage to one or all of their competitors.

After the first auction is complete, drafting begins.

Figure 5.10

Sample Story Sabotages

❖ Require other Writers to develop a protagonist who is an animal or a personified object.

❖ Require other Writers to incorporate a minimum number of settings or perspectives.

❖ Require other Writers to employ a circular narrative.

❖ Require other Writers to "force" certain challenge items into their stories such as a hubcap or a bizarre line of dialogue.

❖ Allow the auction winner to assign the other Writers one of several story mashups featuring unusual pairings such as dystopian meets Virginia Woolf.

❖ Allow the auction winner to assign certain seasons or times of day to the other Writers as the only setting they can employ in their narrative.

❖ Restrict the genre so only the auction winner can write in standard prose. Everyone else must write in another genre such as verse, epistolary format, graphic novel, etc.

Rounds 2 and 3 (15 minutes each):
Repeat the "Round 1" process (minus the story prompt) two more times during the drafting stage, being sure to move through the auction rounds quickly (take no more than two minutes per auction to maximize drafting time). Each round should *total* (including the auction time), 15 minutes.

When students have two minutes remaining in the final round, be sure to give a two-minute warning so they can wind their stories down to a workable conclusion. Consider having a timer going on the board so all competitive teams can easily check their pacing as they draft.

Scoring (30 minutes):
Each competitive team will now serve as judges for another heat. Assemble two different competitive teams together face-to-face and provide scoring sheets to each student. If the story prompts were not identical across heats, the host for each competitive team will provide the story prompt (but not the challenge elements) to the scoring team.

Each narrative will be introduced by the host anonymously as, for example, Student A, Student B, etc. Judges will score the work quickly based on the criteria identified on the rubric, a sample of which can be found in **Figure 5.11**. Once all the narratives have been read and scored, the host will inform the judges how many purchase tokens each student has remaining (e.g., Student A has five purchase tokens remaining, Student B has two, etc.) The purchase tokens will then be added to their rubric score and the final tally will be calculated. The competitor with the highest score wins that heat.

The process repeats for the other competitive team until all students have earned their scores.

Declaring the Victors (5 minutes):
In the final five minutes, scores for all heats will be posted to the board and the final tally will be calculated to determine the winning Team. Once the winning Team has been declared, any remaining time will be used to celebrate other "wins" such as the most original, most creative, or silliest story elements they encountered during this activity, regardless of how those pieces were ultimately scored.

Figure 5.11

Story Saboteur Judge's Score Card

Sample Name:

Criteria	😒 1	😐 2	🙂 3	😃 4	😎 5
Overall Narrative On a purely emotional level, how does this narrative make you feel?					
Alignment to Prompt Based on your understanding of the original story prompt (genre, required elements, etc.), how closely does this narrative align with the assigned prompt?					
Cohesion Overall, how cohesive does this story feel? Does the story flow relatively seamlessly, or are there places where the narrative feels jumpy, incomplete, or overly confusing?					
Artfulness How did the Writer's use of style, organization, and other artful techniques affect the narrative?					

Narrative Score: _____

+ Remaining Purchase Tokens: _____

= Total Score

Differentiate

To Support:

For younger/struggling learners, select your competitive teams carefully to ensure that students are grouped with others who are roughly equal in writing strengths and/or that they are grouped with students who are most likely to be supportive, even during competitive play. Select your sabotage elements carefully as well, differentiating the level of challenge for each sabotage to the needs of your class. The goal is to provide a challenge that is *just* beyond the reach of the average Writer in your class, not a challenge that is so far beyond their current abilities as to be unmanageable. Think about what a writing "stretch" looks like in each of your classes and design your sabotages accordingly.

To Challenge:

Challenge experienced or advanced learners by ratcheting up the difficulty of the sabotage elements. Generally speaking, the more specific and narrow the required elements that must be included, the more difficult it will be for students to revise their writing effectively. Consider the skills and concepts you are only just beginning to explore in your classes at this point and use them as the inspiration for your challenges. As with younger or struggling learners, the challenge level should always be *just* beyond (as opposed to well beyond) their current skill level, but what you consider a "stretch" for your students will be dependent upon the individual learners in your classroom.

Suggested Unit Integration:

This activity pairs well with a number of instructional units, from genre study, to close reading, to lessons on the writing process. However, because of the competitive nature of this lesson as well as the challenge level it involves, I recommend holding this lesson until at least the semester mark of the school year. This will allow students to gain a strong enough understanding of the foundational skills to find success with this activity and will also allow students to get a sense of the other Writers in the classroom in order to recognize and understand their unique strengths.

If students do not yet understand the foundational skills and/or if they do not sufficiently know their classmates as Writers, they will not be as successful with this activity as we ultimately want them to be. In addition, the farther along you are in the school year, the more difficult you can make the sabotage elements. Personally, I prefer to teach this lesson at the very end of the school year (hence its placement in this book) because it can be designed to serve as a great review for a wide range of academic skills. In addition, because of its competitive nature, delivering this lesson at the end of the school year ensures teachers have had sufficient time to develop the supportive and playful classroom culture necessary for this lesson to be a success.

Extension Activity:

- *Creative Writing Publication Piece—Personal Narrative:* Using this activity as inspiration, students should write a Publication Piece Personal Narrative in which they explore a time in their lives (a moment, an event, etc.) where everything went wrong and, as a result, something wonderful came about. In other words, how did they benefit from what initially appeared to be a disaster?

- *Literary Analysis:* Provide students with poems, short stories, excerpts from longer texts, or full-length novels as desired. Then, ask students to "score" that text using the same rubric they used for this activity. Once they have scored that text, they should conduct a literary analysis that explains and justifies the score, being sure to bring in specific textual evidence to support their findings.

- *Writing Portfolio—Self-Reflection:* Similar to the Literary Analysis activity above, ask students to select one of their own earlier Publication Pieces and score that work against the same rubric as the one used for this activity. Once they have scored their work, they should conduct a self-reflection analysis that explains and justifies the score, identifying areas of strengths and areas they would like to target for improvement going forward, being sure to use specific textual evidence to support their findings (see **Figure 5.12** for sample instructions for this extension activity).

Figure 5.12

Extension Activity: Self-Reflection

Congratulations on reaching the end of the school year! You have worked hard this year and have learned many new skills, techniques, and approaches to writing. As a result, you have become a thoughtful Writer, recognizing the impact of authorial choice on meaning.

In our most recent Writing Wednesday lesson, you had a chance to review and score the work of other Writers, exploring the piece both in reaction to the emotions it stirred up for you, as well as in connection with the effectiveness of the overall narrative.

As you prepare to embark upon your next adventures, take a moment to recognize and reflect upon your own growth as a Writer.

Directions: Select any one of your previous Publication Pieces (the polished, rather than the draft, document). Then, using the same rubric you used to score the competing team's work during the *Story Saboteur* lesson, score your own piece.

Once you have scored your work, write a one- to two-paragraph analysis that explains and justifies your score, identifying both areas of strength and areas you would like to target for improvement going forward. Be sure to provide specific textual evidence from your Publication Piece to support your analysis.

Conclude your analysis with a reflection that explores what you have learned about the writing process overall during the course of this school year, how you might use this knowledge when tackling writing tasks in the future, and how confident you feel in your ability to review and improve your own writing before finalizing each piece for publication going forward.

QUARTER 4 CELEBRATION DAY

Congratulations on reaching the end of the school year!

By this point in their Writer's journey, students will be ready to explore their earlier drafts with an eye towards potential, as opposed to critique. In addition, they will have had a chance to work with their Team for months, learning each other's strengths and talents. Therefore, this final Celebration Day is designed to celebrate the larger writing community that has been developed over the course of the year: both the individuals and the Teams.

This suggested Celebration Day activity connects to student learning this quarter by requiring that each individual Publication Piece focus on a narrow window of life, as opposed to offering a sweeping look at some larger universal topic and by challenging students to control their style elements to shape the reader's understanding. It also reminds students to seek the potential in their writing by forcing them to explore a previous draft and engage in the Writing Process to makeover their earlier work into something new. Finally, it requires students to recognize that everyone has something valuable to add to our understanding of the world, encouraging students to "steal" the vision of others in order to give voice to their own world, engaging in writing as a conversation, rather than a lecture.

Figure 5.13

VISION AND VOICE

Congratulations on reaching your final Celebration Day event!

Today, we will celebrate the progress you have made over the course of the year as individual Writers and as part of a larger writing community. Therefore, for this activity, you will showcase your best work, both as an individual and as a Team.

This multi-step process has been broken down below:

STEP 1:

Individually, explore your Writer's Notebook to identify the draft that has the most potential as a Publication Piece. This may be the draft you selected for the *Writing Makeover* activity or you may select an entirely different draft. However, you must select a draft from an earlier writing to revise, as opposed to developing an entirely new narrative. Develop a revision plan for this piece and share your ideas with your Writing Team, requesting and accepting feedback as appropriate to help you design your best work.

STEP 2:

As a Team, review the Publication Piece selections of each Team member, listening carefully to their specific writing goals and providing feedback and suggestions to guide them on their revision journey.

Then, **as a Team**, select one element from *each* Team member's work that must be woven into everyone's individual revision piece. In other words, although each individual piece will be different and unique from the others, everyone's work will reflect and celebrate elements of the work produced by the entire Team.

STEP 3:

Individually, take your selected piece through the revision process, checking in with the Team at various points to ensure everyone's work continues to reflect the selected shared elements as the revision process continues.

Each individual Publication Piece must include

- ❏ A focus on a narrow "window" of life
- ❏ Deliberate and thoughtful stylistic choices which are intended to shape the reader's understanding, and
- ❏ The shared elements from the other Team Members, as determined by the Team in Step 2.

Assessment Requirements:

Group Presentation: Each Team will present their process for completing this activity, including a reflection of how individual members selected their Publication Pieces, which elements from each member were chosen to be incorporated into all of the pieces, why those elements were selected, and how each member used those elements to shape their individual pieces.

Individual Submission: Each Team member will submit their individual creation and self-reflection for an assessment score. As part of the reflection, be sure to address

- ➤ How the brainstorming stage of the activity informed the selection of your own unique narrative
- ➤ What window into life you were hoping to create
- ➤ How and why you used stylistic elements to control your reader's experience, and
- ➤ How you chose to weave the required elements from the other members' work into your piece and how your choices helped support your writing goals.

Your opinion matters!

I recognize that you could have . . .

> Slept in
> Gone for a bike ride
> Cooked brunch
> Taken a walk
> Gone shopping
> Played a game
> Dined out
> Watched a movie
> Nibbled on dessert

But instead, you read my book.
Wow. Thanks!

As a busy teacher myself, I know how valuable time—especially downtime—is. I sincerely hope you feel reading this book was a good use of your time.

If you do, please leave a review to let others know why reading this book is better than all the other cool things you could have been doing. If not, please let me know how upcoming books can be more helpful to you going forward.

Share your story and become part of the Writing Wednesday community:

❖ Leave a review at amazon.com, barnesandnoble.com, or alexandritepublishing.com

❖ Mention this book / follow us on social media:

> ❖ Facebook
> ❖ Instagram
> ❖ LinkedIn
> ❖ Pinterest

❖ Share Writing Wednesday success stories on social media and tag us: @alexandritepublishing / #WritingWednesdaysWork

❖ Join our Hidden Gems Membership program

❖ Become a guest contributor to The AlexandWriter Blog

❖ Or email me through my publisher at: info@alexandritepublishing.com with your questions or comments

References

10 Things I Hate About You. Gill Junger, et al. Touchstone Pictures, 1999.

Abbott, Bud, and Lou Costello. "Who's on First?" *The Abbott and Costello Show*, 1944.

Alvarez, Julia. *In the Time of the Butterflies*. Algonquin Books, 2010.

Apple, Fiona. "Sleep to Dream." *Tidal*, Work Records, Columbia Records, 1996.

Armstrong, Louis. "Black and Blue." 1929.

Blake, William. "The Lamb by William Blake." *Poetry Foundation*, https://www.poetryfoundation.org/poems/43670/the-lamb-56d222765a3e1.

---. "The Tyger by William Blake." *Poetry Foundation*, https://www.poetryfoundation.org/poems/43687/the-tyger.

Brontë, Emily. *Wuthering Heights*. Borders Group Inc., 2009.

Brown, Alton, host. *Cutthroat Kitchen*. Food Network, Embassy Row, 2013-2017.

Cash, Johnny. "Personal Jesus." *Remixes* 2:81-11, Mute, 2011.

Chavez, Felicia Rose. *The Anti-Racist Writing Workshop: How to Decolonize the Creative Classroom*. Haymarket Books, 2021.

Counting Crows and Vanessa Carlton. "Big Yellow Taxi." *Hard Candy*, Geffen, 2003.

Dali, Salvador. *The Persistence of Memory*. 1931, Museum of Modern Art, New York.

Depeche Mode. "Personal Jesus." *Violator*, Mute, 1989.

Diamond, Neil. "Red Red Wine." *Just for You*, Bang, 1967.

Ellison, Ralph Waldo. *Invisible Man*. Vintage International, 1980.

Fieri, Guy. *Guy's Grocery Games*. Food Network, Knuckle Sandwich Production Company, 2013-present.

Flower, Linda S., & John R. Hayes. "Problem-Solving Strategies and the Writing Process." *College English*, vol. 39, no. 4, 1977, pp. 449-461.

Gallagher, Kelly. "Moving beyond the 4 x 4 Classroom." *Kelly Gallagher*, Kelly Gallagher, 24 Feb. 2018, http://www.kellygallagher.org/kellys-blog/2015/7/14/moving-beyond-the-4-x-4-classroom.

Graham, Steve. "Changing How Writing Is Taught." *Review of Research in Education*, vol. 43, no. 1, Mar. 2019, pp. 277–303, doi:**10.3102/0091732X18821125**.

Hirano, Keiichiro. *At the End of the Matinee*. Amazon Publishing, 2021.

Houston, Whitney. "I Will Always Love You." *The Bodyguard*, Arista, 1992.

Hovan, Gretchen. "Writing For a Built-in Audience: Writing Groups in the Middle School Classroom." *Voices from the Middle*, vol. 20, no. 2, 2012, pp. 49-53.

Human League. "Don't You Want Me." *Dare*, Virgin, 1981.

Jackson, Shirley, and Jonathan Lethem. *We Have Always Lived in the Castle*. Penguin Books, 2021.

James, H. (n.d.). *Preface to The Portrait of a Lady*. The Literature Network. http://www.online-literature.com/henry_james/portrait_lady/0/.

Jones, Gloria. "Tainted Love." Champion, 1965.

Kahlo, Frida. *The Two Fridas*. 1939, Museo de Arte Moderno, Mexico City.

Lakeside. "Fantastic Voyage." *Fantastic Voyage*, SOLAR, 1981.

LaVette Bettye. "Sleep to Dream." *I've Got My Own Hell to Raise*, ANTI, 2005.

Li-Young Lee, "A Story." *The City in Which I Love You*. 1990.

Liu, Ken. "The Paper Menagerie." *Head of Zeus*, 2016.

Magritte, Rene. *The Son of Man*. 1964, Private Collection.

McLachlan, Sarah. "Fallen." *Afterglow*, Arista Nettwerk, 2003.

Metallica. "Unforgiven." *Metallica*, Elektra, 1991.

Mitchell, Joni. "Big Yellow Taxi." *Ladies of the Canyon*, Reprise, 1970.

Munch, Edvard. *The Scream*. 1893, National Gallery and Munch Museum, Oslo.

Murray, Donald M. "Teach Writing as a Process Not Product." *The Leaflet*, vol. 71, no. 3, 1972, pp. 11-14.

National Governors Association Center for Best Practices & Council of Chief State School Officers (2010). "Common Core State Standards for English language arts and literacy in history/social studies, science, and technical subjects." Washington, DC, 2015.

Parton, Dolly. "I Will Always Love You." *Jolene*, RCA Victor, 1974.

Patchett, Ann. *Bel Canto: A Novel*. Harper Perennial, 2005.

Poe, Edgar Allan. *The Fall of the House of Usher: and Other Tales*. Vintage, 2010.

Ratner, Vaddey. *In the Shadow of the Banyan*. Simon & Schuster UK, 2013.

Robinson, Edwin Arlington. "Richard Cory by Edwin Arlington Robinson." *Poetry Foundation*, Poetry Foundation, https://www.poetryfoundation.org/poems/44982/richard-cory.

Rushdie, Salman. *Haroun and the Sea of Stories*. Penguin Books, 2020.

Scott, Dan, et al. "The Bull by Pablo Picasso." *Draw Paint Academy*, 7 May 2021, https://drawpaintacademy.com/the-bull/.

Shakespeare, William, et al. "'Othello.'" *Tragedies, Volume 1*, Knopf, New York, NY, 1992, pp. 153–280.

---, et al. "'The Taming of the Shrew.'" *Comedies, Volume 1*, Knopf, New York, 1995, pp. 79-187.

Shelley, Mary Wollstonecraft, et al. *Frankenstein, or, the Modern Prometheus: The Original Two-Volume Novel of 1816-1817 from the Bodleian Library Manuscripts*. Vintage Books, 2009.

Smith, Stevie. "Not Waving but Drowning." *Poetry Foundation*, Poetry Foundation, https://www.poetryfoundation.org/poems/46479/not-waving-but-drowning.

Soft Cell. "Tainted Love." *Non-Stop Erotic Cabaret*, Some Bizarre Sire, Warner Brothers Records, 1981.

Steinbeck, John. *The Grapes of Wrath*. Penguin, 2008.

Tchaikovsky, Peter Ilich, 1840-1893. *The Swan Lake Ballet*. New York: Vanguard, 1967.

UB40. "Red Red Wine." *Labour of Love*, DEP, A&M, Virgin, 1983.

van Gogh, Vincent. *Sorrowing Old Man (At Eternity's Gate)*. 1890, Kröller-Müller Museum, Otterlo.

---. *The Starry Night*. 1889, Museum of Modern Art, New York.

Warhol, Andy. *Campbell's Soup Cans*. 1962, Museum of Modern Art, New York.

Wiesel, Elie. *Night*. Translated by Marion Wiesel, Hill & Wang, 2006.

---. *Night*. Translated by Stella Rodway, Bantam Books, 1989.

Wood, Grant. *American Gothic*. 1930, Art Institute of Chicago, Chicago.

Woolf, Virginia, and Susan Dick. "An Unwritten Novel." *The Complete Shorter Fiction of Virginia Woolf*. Harvest Book, 2006.

Zusak, Markus. *The Book Thief*. Picador/Pan Macmillan Australia, 2019.

Bibliography

#TeachLivingPoets, /. *#Teachlivingpoets: Complicating the Canon and Empowering Students Through Poetry*. 27 Feb. 2022, https://teachlivingpoets.com/.

"10 Emerging Black Male Artists to Collect." *BLACK ART IN AMERICA™*, 19 June 2018, https://www.blackartinamerica.com/index.php/2018/06/19/10-emerging-black-male-artists-to-collect/.

10 Things I Hate About You. Gill Junger, et al. Touchstone Pictures, 1999.

Abbott, Bud and Lou Costello. "Who's on First?" *The Abbott and Costello Show*, 1944.

Alexandra. "21 Instagram Theme Ideas Using Preview App (+ Editing Tips)." *Preview App*, 3 Jan. 2022, https://thepreviewapp.com/15-instagram-theme-ideas-preview-app/.

Alvarez, Julia. *In the Time of the Butterflies*. Algonquin Books, 2010.

Apple, Fiona. "Sleep to Dream." *Tidal*, Work Records, Columbia Records, 1996.

Armstrong, Louis. "Black and Blue." 1929.

"Art News Magazine." *Art & Object | News from the Art World*, https://www.artandobject.com/.

"Asian Art Museum." *Education*, III Dec. 2021, https://education.asianart.org/.

Beers, G. Kylene, and Robert E. Probst. *Disrupting Thinking: Why How We Read Matters*. Scholastic Inc., 2017.

Bergland, Christopher. "Why Does Writing By Hand Promote Better and Faster Learning?" *Psychology Today*. https://www.psychologytoday.com/us/blog/the-athletes-way/202107/why-does-writing-hand-promote-better-and-faster-learning

"Best Music Mashup 2020 - Best of Popular Songs." *YouTube*, 6 June 2020, https://www.youtube.com/watch?v=zAQacLrltNY.

Blake, William. "The Lamb by William Blake." *Poetry Foundation*, https://www.poetryfoundation.org/poems/43670/the-lamb-56d222765a3e1.

---. "The Tyger by William Blake." *Poetry Foundation*, https://www.poetryfoundation.org/poems/43687/the-tyger.

Bournes, Micah. *MICAH BOURNES*, https://www.micahbournes.com/home.

Brontë, Emily. *Wuthering Heights*. Borders Group Inc., 2009.

Brown, Alton, host. *Cutthroat Kitchen*. Food Network, Embassy Row, 2013 – 2017.

Cash, Johnny. "Personal Jesus." *Remixes* 2:81-11, Mute, 2011.

Chavez, Felicia Rose. *The Anti-Racist Writing Workshop: How to Decolonize the Creative Classroom*. Haymarket Books, 2021.

"A Community Enriched through the Creative Arts." *ARTfactory*, 4 Mar. 2022, https://www.virginiaartfactory.org/.

Counting Crows and Vanessa Carlton. "Big Yellow Taxi." *Hard Candy*, Geffen, 2003

Culham, Ruth. *The Writing Thief: Using Mentor Texts to Teach the Craft of Writing*. Stenhouse Publishers, 2014.

Dali, Salvador. *The Persistence of Memory*. 1931, Museum of Modern Art, New York.

Dean, Deborah. *Genre Theory: Teaching, Writing, and Being*. National Council of Teachers of English, 2008.

Depeche Mode. "Personal Jesus." *Violator*, Mute, 1989.

Diamond, Neil. "Red Red Wine." *Just for You*, Bang, 1967.

"Docupoetry." *Poetry River*, http://www.poetryriver.org/docupoetry.html.

Ellison, Ralph Waldo. *Invisible Man*. Vintage International, 1980.

Fieri, Guy. *Guy's Grocery Games*. Food Network, Knuckle Sandwich Production Company, 2013 – present.

Flower, Linda S., & John R. Hayes. "Problem-Solving Strategies and the Writing Process." *College English*, vol. 39, no. 4, 1977, pp. 449-461.

"From College to Career Success." *AAC&U*, 16 Dec. 2021, https://www.aacu.org/article/from-college-to-career-success-how-educators-and-employers-talk-about-skills.

Gallagher, Kelly. *Deeper Reading: Comprehending Challenging Texts*, 4-12. Stenhouse Publishers, 2004.

---. "Moving beyond the 4 x 4 Classroom." *Kelly Gallagher*, Kelly Gallagher, 24 Feb. 2018, http://www.kellygallagher.org/kellys-blog/2015/7/14/moving-beyond-the-4-x-4-classroom.

---. *Write like This: Teaching Real-World Writing through Modeling & Mentor Texts*. Stenhouse Publishers, 2011.

Gardner, Janet E., and Joanne Diaz. *Reading and Writing about Literature: A Portable Guide, 4th Ed.*

George, Tom. "Photos by Andrew Kung Celebrating Asian American Pride." *Id*, 1 Dec. 2021, https://i-d.vice.com/en_uk/article/dypgmk/perpetual-foreigner-photography-series.

Graham, Steve. "Changing How Writing Is Taught." Review of Research in Education, vol. 43, no. 1, Mar. 2019, pp. 277–303, doi:**10.3102/0091732X18821125**.

Gray, Dave, et al. *Gamestorming: A Playbook for Innovators, Rulebreakers, and Changemakers*. O'Reilly Media, Inc., USA, 2010.

Hirano, Keiichiro. *At the End of the Matinee*. Amazon Publishing, 2021.

Hirshfield, Jane. *Ten Windows: How Great Poems Transform the World*. Alfred A. Knopf, 2017.

Hooks, Bell. *Teaching to Transgress: Education as the Practice of Freedom*. Routledge, 1996.

Houston, Whitney. "I Will Always Love You." *The Bodyguard*, Arista, 1992.

Hovan, Gretchen. "Writing For a Built-in Audience: Writing Groups in the Middle School Classroom." *Voices from the Middle*, vol. 20, no. 2, 2012, pp. 49-53.

Human League. "Don't You Want Me." *Dare*, Virgin, 1981.

I., Al'ameen Sanusi. "The Psychological Benefits of Writing by Hand." *Medium*, The Writing Cooperative, 28 Dec. 2020, https://writingcooperative.com/the-psychological-benefits-of-writing-by-hand-ffe442ae8dce.

Jackson, Shirley, and Jonathan Lethem. *We Have Always Lived in the Castle*. Penguin Books, 2021.

"Jacob Lawrence: The American Struggle." *Metmuseum.org*, https://www.metmuseum.org/events/programs/met-studies/k12-educator-programs/educator-workshop-jacob-lawrence-fall?fbclid=IwAR1LIhAK7C6cPEYOoW-RZ2p3LDYVyR17Xp892t6yrmzwMHvooIJ_zepO_tY.

James, H. (n.d.). *Preface to The Portrait of a Lady*. The Literature Network. http://www.online-literature.com/henry_james/portrait_lady/0/.

Jones, Gloria. "Tainted Love." Champion, 1965.

Kahlo, Frida. *The Two Fridas*. 1939, Museo de Arte Moderno, Mexico City.

Kaner, Sam. *Facilitator's Guide to Participatory Decision-Making*. Jossey-Bass, 2014.

Lakeside. "Fantastic Voyage." *Fantastic Voyage*, SOLAR, 1981.

LaVette Bettye. "Sleep to Dream." *I've Got My Own Hell to Raise*, ANTI, 2005.

Lemov, Doug, et al. *Reading Reconsidered: A Practical Guide to Rigorous Literacy Instruction*. John Wiley & Sons, 2016.

Li-Young Lee, "A Story." *The City in Which I Love You*. 1990.

Lindaman, Dana. *History Lessons: How Textbooks from around the World Portray U.S. History*. New Press, 2006.

Liu, Ken. "The Paper Menagerie." Head of Zeus, 2016.

Magritte, Rene. *The Son of Man*. 1964, Private Collection.

McLachlan, Sarah. "Fallen." *Afterglow*, Arista Nettwerk, 2003.

Metallica. "Unforgiven." *Metallica*, Elektra, 1991.

Mitchell, Joni. "Big Yellow Taxi." *Ladies of the Canyon*, Reprise, 1970.

"Moma." *The Museum of Modern Art*, https://www.moma.org/.

Morenberg, Max, and Jeffrey Sommers. *The Writer's Options: Lessons in Style and Arrangement*. Pearson Longman, 2008.

Muhammad, Gholdy, and Bettina L. Love. *Cultivating Genius: An Equity Framework for Culturally and Historically Responsive Literacy*. Scholastic, 2020.

Munch, Edvard. *The Scream*. 1893, National Gallery and Munch Museum, Oslo.

Murray, Donald M. "Teach Writing as a Process Not Product." *The Leaflet*, vol. 71, no. 3, 1972, pp. 11-14.

National Governors Association Center for Best Practices & Council of Chief State School Officers (2010). "Common Core State Standards for English language arts and literacy in history/social studies, science, and technical subjects." Washington, DC, 2015.

Neubert, Gloria A., and Elizabeth A. Wilkins. *Putting It All Together: The Directed Reading Lesson in the Secondary Content Classroom*. Pearson, 2004.

Parton, Dolly. "I Will Always Love You." *Jolene*, RCA Victor, 1974.

Patchett, Ann. *Bel Canto: A Novel*. Harper Perennial, 2005.

Poe, Edgar Allan. *The Fall of the House of Usher: and Other Tales*. Vintage, 2010.

Potter, Cathy. "Windows and Mirrors and Sliding Glass Doors: Ensuring Students See Themselves and Others in Literature." *Institute for Humane Education*, 30 Sept. 2020, https://humaneeducation.org/windows-and-mirrors-and-sliding-glass-doors-ensuring-students-see-themselves-and-others-in-literature/.

"Project Zero's Thinking Routine Toolbox." *PZ's Thinking Routines Toolbox | Project Zero*, http://www.pz.harvard.edu/thinking-routines.

Ratner, Vaddey. *In the Shadow of the Banyan*. Simon & Schuster UK, 2013.

"Rethinking 'Content': The Four Truths." *National Parks Service*, U.S. Department of the Interior, https://mylearning.nps.gov/library-resources/rethinking-content-four-truths/.

Robinson, Edwin Arlington. "Richard Cory by Edwin Arlington Robinson." *Poetry Foundation*, Poetry Foundation, https://www.poetryfoundation.org/poems/44982/richard-cory.

Rothstein, Dan, et al. *Make Just One Change: Teach Students to Ask Their Own Questions*. Harvard Education Press, 2018.

Rushdie, Salman. *Haroun and the Sea of Stories*. Penguin Books, 2020.

Scott, Dan, et al. "The Bull by Pablo Picasso." *Draw Paint Academy*, 7 May 2021, https://drawpaintacademy.com/the-bull/.

Sebranek, Patrick. *Writers Inc: A Student Handbook for Writing & Learning*. Write Source, 1996.

Shakespeare, William, et al. "'Othello.'" *Tragedies, Volume 1*, Knopf, New York, NY, 1992, pp. 153–280.

---, et al. "'The Taming of the Shrew.'" *Comedies, Volume 1*, Knopf, New York, 1995, pp. 79-187.

Shelley, Mary Wollstonecraft, et al. *Frankenstein, or, the Modern Prometheus: The Original Two-Volume Novel of 1816-1817 from the Bodleian Library Manuscripts*. Vintage Books, 2009.

Smith, Michael W., and Jeffrey D. Wilhelm. *Getting It Right: Fresh Approaches to Teaching Grammar, Usage, and Correctness*. Scholastic, 2007.

Smith, Stevie. "Not Waving but Drowning." *Poetry Foundation*, https://www.poetryfoundation.org/poems/46479/not-waving-but-drowning.

Soft Cell. "Tainted Love." *Non-Stop Erotic Cabaret*, Some Bizarre Sire, Warner Brothers Records, 1981.

Steinbeck, John. *The Grapes of Wrath*. Penguin, 2008.

Tchaikovsky, Peter Ilich, 1840-1893. *The Swan Lake Ballet*. New York: Vanguard, 1967.

UB40. "Red Red Wine." *Labour of Love*, DEP, A&M, Virgin, 1983.

Urbanski, Cynthia D. *Using the Workshop Approach in the High School English Classroom: Modeling Effective Writing, Reading, and Thinking Strategies for Student Success*. Corwin Press, 2006.

van Gogh, Vincent. *Sorrowing Old Man (At Eternity's Gate)*. 1890, Kröller-Müller Museum, Otterlo.

---. *The Starry Night*. 1889, Museum of Modern Art, New York.

Warhol, Andy. *Campbell's Soup Cans*. 1962, Museum of Modern Art, New York.

Wiesel, Elie. *Night*. Translated by Marion Wiesel, Hill & Wang, 2006.

---. *Night*. Translated by Stella Rodway, Bantam Books, 1989.

Wood, Grant. *American Gothic*. 1930, Art Institute of Chicago, Chicago.

Woolf, Virginia, and Susan Dick. "An Unwritten Novel." *The Complete Shorter Fiction of Virginia Woolf*. Harvest Book, 2006.

"Write Center." *WRITE CENTER*, https://www.writecenter.org/.

"Writing, Technology and Teens." *Pew Research Center: Internet, Science & Tech*, Pew Research Center, 30 May 2020, https://www.pewresearch.org/internet/2008/04/24/writing-technology-and-teens/.

Zusak, Markus. *The Book Thief*. Picador/Pan Macmillan Australia, 2019.

Index

Artfulness

M

N

O

P

Q

R

Z